*f*P

BULLSEYE!

HITTING YOUR STRATEGIC TARGETS
THROUGH HIGH-IMPACT MEASUREMENT

•

WILLIAM A. SCHIEMANN

AND

JOHN H. LINGLE

THE FREE PRESS

THE FREE PRESS
A Division of Simon & Schuster Inc.
1230 Avenue of the Americas
New York, NY 10020

Designed by MM Design 2000, Inc.

Manufactured in the United States of America

10   9   8   7   6   5   4   3   2   1

Library of Congress Cataloging-in-Publication Data

Schiemann, William.
    Bullseye! : hitting your strategic targets through high-impact
measurement / William A. Schiemann and John H. Lingle.
        p.   cm.
    Includes bibliographical references and index.
    ISBN 0–684–85452–X
    1. Organizational effectiveness—Evaluation.   2. Performance—
Evaluation.   I. Lingle, John H.   II. Title.
HD56.25.S35   1999
658.4'012—dc21   99–41260
                                                          CIP

ISBN 0–684–85452–X

From Bill to:

Mom & Dad, and Valeria for their love and support

From John to:

Tom and Peter for the many lessons learned

ACKNOWLEDGMENTS

Over the years we have received a good deal of advice about writing a book. One of our former mentors, Joel Moses, told us not to publish a book until we had something to say. Another advisor observed that writing a book is even more serious than getting married—once a book is published, it cannot be undone!

This book has been three years in the writing and nearly two decades in its conceptual evolution. We have watched numerous trends come and go and looked for the underlying element that would really make a difference to tomorrow's organization. In producing this work, we hope we have made a meaningful contribution.

In the course of our journey we have been inspired by many people with whom we have worked. First, we would both like to thank our respective graduate school advisors, George Graen, Charles Hulin, and Thomas Ostrom, who provided inspiring tutelage in psychology and measurement disciplines.

Our early work at Opinion Research Corporation deepened our understanding of measurement. The work of thought leaders Jim Heskett, John Kotter, Bradley Gale, Edgar Schein, Robert Kaplan, David Norton, Stan Davis, and C. K. Prahalad has also been important to our development.

Our interest has always been in how ideas can move reality. In this regard, we have been very fortunate to work with exceptional organizational leaders, including William Crouse, Lawrence Marsiello, Anthony Rucci, and Donald Tornberg. They have been superb role models of thinking in action.

We are indebted to a number of colleagues at Metrus Group and friends who have helped with the collection of research data, case information, and ideas that helped us in explicating our thoughts. These included Mary Azzolini, Michael Barr, Kent Carson, Joe Kilbride, Brian Morgan, Klaus Oebel, Carolyn Ott, Russ Scalpone, James Shillaber, and David Zatz.

As we developed and redeveloped our themes over the past year, we have been grateful to have an outstanding group of reviewers who have provided invaluable insights, including Bill Hunnex, James Heskett, Ray Grymski, and Peter M. Tobia as well as William Crouse, Lawrence Marsiello and Donald Tornberg.

It would not have been possible to produce this book without outstanding administrative and editorial support that included Maryellen Kohl, our right arm; Heather Skiles; Norma Bugle; and Sharon McTague-Hall. Finally, we want to thank the entire team of Metrus Group professionals, present and past, for shaping our ideas and for their patience and support during a challenging period.

Three individuals deserve special attention. First, this book would not have been possible without the support, cajoling, and inspiration of Peter M. Tobia, our literary agent and loyal friend. He had the foresight to see what was possible, and to push us to accomplish it. Second, we both owe a great deal of gratitude to our wonderful spouses, Nancy Lingle and Valeria Schiemann, who have been enormously patient when we were not, and who provided us with tremendous support throughout this marathon adventure.

CONTENTS

PREFACE

Bullseye! is about understanding and resolving the paradox of measurement. This paradox has been set up on the one hand by widespread rhetoric which extols the virtues of measuring business results. On the other hand, surprisingly few companies go beyond the rhetoric to put in place a disciplined approach for measuring the key nonfinancial, strategic performance areas that are crucial to an organization's success. Why is this the case? And how can organizations go about the task of putting in place a strategic measurement system that drives organizational change and business results?

We begin by examining "measurement-managed organizations"—those role-model companies that engage the power of measurement to propel them forward to their goals. What does it mean to be measurement managed? Are these companies really more successful than their non measurement-managed counterparts? Or, as we ask in Chapters 1 and 2, is measurement worth the effort? The measurement paradox would have been easily resolved had we discovered that measurement is not as valuable as popular opinion would lead us to believe.

As you will see, we found nothing to contradict some of the widely extolled advantages of measurement. In fact, we discovered in a number of different studies that measurement-managed companies not only perform better financially compared to their non measurement-managed counterparts—an average three-year ROI of 80 percent versus an average ROI of 45 percent—but they exhibit superior performance on a number of cultural dimensions that are likely to become increasingly important for success in the twenty-first century. Once we examined the data, it became clear that measurement-managed organizations have discovered a weapon that should keep them competitive well into the next century.

In Chapter 3 we look at a key piece of the measurement paradox by examining the deterrents that prevent organizations from doing a better job at strategic measurement. In Chapter 4 we discuss the process required for an organization to become a high-performing, measurement-managed organization.

And herein lies the crux of the paradox: There are a number of powerful forces that conspire against changing the measurement system of any organization. Overcoming these forces requires a systematic change process that eludes many organizations. The failure to effect change has created the paradox in which there are so many companies with ineffective measurement systems in an environment that widely extols measurement but contains only a relatively small number of high performers.

At the heart of the book, in Chapters 5 through 8, we use a case study to describe in fair detail a four-phase process that can successfully transform your company into a measurement-managed organization. The process, while challenging, enables an organization to realize rapid improvements as the measurement system is integrated into its day-to-day operations.

We conclude in Chapter 9 with the seven deadly myths that derail measurement effectiveness, and we provide suggestions on how to puncture these myths to achieve effectiveness as a measurement-managed organization.

Our main objectives in writing *Bullseye! Hitting Your Strategic Targets Through High-Impact Measurement* are to examine the role that strategic measurement plays in creating sustained business results and to provide guidance on how to make strategic measurement work for your organization.

This book is intended for organizational leaders, whether they are at headquarters or in strategic business units, divisions, or plants. Any senior line or staff executive interested in making change happen and producing results should find take-home value in the pages that follow.

Simplicity and speed are essential competitive qualities. Building Gothic monuments of measurement may satisfy the theorists, but this does little for executives on the firing line who must act, now. Serious readers should be able to make significant improvements within three months. Major change should be implemented within a year. If changes to your strategic measurement system do not show significant improvement within six to twelve months, they probably never will.

PART I

RESOLVING THE
MEASUREMENT PARADOX

Measurement is the first step that leads to control and eventually to improvement. If you can't measure something, you can't understand it. If you can't understand it, you can't control it. If you can't control it, you can't improve it.[1]

H. James Harrington

T he business literature abounds with examples of organizational turnarounds that support Mr. Harrington's observation. For example, between 1992 and 1993 Sears's Merchandising Group went from a $3 billion loss to a $752 million profit.[2] A key element of this successful turnaround, as documented in the *Harvard Business Review,* was the development of a measurement system that tied employee job satisfaction and commitment directly to customer retention and improvements in store revenue. Today, Sears has executive compensation linked to measures of employee commitment and customer satisfaction, as well as revenue.

The turnaround at Continental Airlines provides a parallel example. In his book, *From Worst to First,*[3] Gordon Bethune chronicles the impressive turnaround of a near-bankrupt airline. In 1994 Continental Airlines had not made a profit for ten years and was dead last among major airlines in on-time percentage, and first in mishandled baggage and customer complaints. In 1995 the company made $202 million, beginning a string of eleven profitable quarters. In May 1996, customers surveyed by *Frequent Flyer* magazine and J. D. Power and Associates voted Continental the best airline for flights of five hundred miles or more. Again, a key element of this two-year turnaround was a rebuilt measurement system and the detailed communication of key strategic performance indicators to employees throughout the organization.

With documented success stories like these, it is hardly surprising that in 1998 the Conference Board registered twice the expected attendees at its national conference on strategic measurement. You just can't argue with the power of measurement to drive organizational success, or be surprised by the interest of executives in improving their measurement system.

Or can you?

If the power of measurement is so obvious—and if executives are focused on improving their measurement systems:

Why is it that in a recent study only 54 percent of the executives polled said that their leadership team had a well-defined and balanced set of strategic measures?[4] Why is it that another recent study found that only 29 percent of the interviewed executives said they would bet their job on the measures of customer satisfaction they had available to them; only 16 percent said they would bet their job on the measures they had of employee performance?[5]

Why is it that the very same study also found that fewer than one in five executives reported that their company regularly tracks measures related to innovation and change in their organization?

Why, despite study after study showing that employee job satisfaction and commitment drive service quality, do fewer than one in four executives report that their company uses employee satisfaction and commitment measures to predict customer satisfaction and financial performance?

What's going on? If measurement is universally accepted as crucial to business success, why aren't executives measuring in a timely and effective manner more of the things that matter?

Take the following thirty-second test about your own organization:

First, put down the book and make a note of the few dozen or so things that really matter to the long-term success of your business. Be thorough. Sure, revenue generation is critical, but what else matters? Is it the satisfaction of your customers? Is it the commitment and loyalty of your employees? Is it improving work force competencies? Regulatory issues? Labor issues? Recruiting new talent? Whatever it is, write down the top twelve items that really matter to the *long-term* success of your business.

Do you have your list?

O.K., make a list of the measures you talked about in your last quarterly business review meeting. Did you talk about the revenue numbers? What other numbers did you talk about? Measures of customer loyalty? Competencies? Regulatory issues?

Now, how well do the two lists match up? Are you reviewing on a regular basis measures of the dozen things that really matter to your organization's long-term success? Or is your organization yet one more example of the measurement paradox in which there is a chasm between the rhetoric espousing the importance of measurement and a reality that denies it?

Let us now explore the paradox of measurement and how to go about resolving it.

CHAPTER 1

MEASUREMENT MANAGEMENT: WHAT IS IT AND IS IT WORTH THE EFFORT?

W e have been long-standing advocates of the power of measurement. In the 1970s and 1980s only a handful of companies were relying heavily upon nonfinancial and nonoperational measures such as employee perception and organizational "climate" surveys to make tough strategic business decisions. United Parcel Service of America, Inc., for example, asked us to help it develop a labor satisfaction index that executives could use to identify union voting districts with the greatest labor discontent.

Such companies were the exception, however. Today, one indicator of the value of this type of measurement is the fact that many of the leading Fortune 100 companies, such as Sears, Roebuck and Co., FDX Corporation (formerly Federal Express), The Walt Disney Company, Inc., General Electric Company, The Procter & Gamble Company, and Johnson & Johnson—to name just a few—use a balanced set of nonfinancial and nonoperational measures to help manage their business. In the process, measurement has been transformed to balanced *strategic measurement—* an important new management tool for driving the implementation of business strategy.

Over the years, we have had firsthand experience with a number of companies that have used strategic measurement to help drive rapid change in their business. For example, from 1988 to 1991, under the leadership of William Crouse, Johnson & Johnson's Ortho Diagnostic Systems, Inc., now Ortho-Clinical Diagnostics, saw sales and profits soar. A key component of this change, as chronicled in *Management Review*,[1] was a revitalization of the company's measurement system, including the employee survey process.

More recently, we were involved in helping a major unit of The CIT Group, Inc., a global financial service company, improve its performance through the redesign of its strategic measurement system. In a little over a year the company reenergized its operations and achieved a 45 percent return on equity and 7 percent revenue growth in a no-growth market niche. During this period the company managed to reduce customer defections by 50 percent, while employee ratings of teamwork, senior leadership, implementation of new ideas, and performance management all improved by more than 18 percent.

While our involvement with these and other organizations has convinced us of the power of measurement, skeptics would argue that there is always the possibility that factors other than measurement were responsible for the performance improvements cited in our examples. In addition, when you consider the fact that many smart executives are not yet measuring performance beyond the financial and operational areas, could it be that measurement in the other areas just doesn't matter that much?

IN SEARCH OF CONFIRMATION

Our belief in the importance of strategic measurement led us several years ago to embark on a more systematic study of the value of measurement. If our experiences were valid, it seemed to us that we should be able to demonstrate more convincingly that companies doing a good job at measurement are more successful than those that are not.

To investigate—and measure—the impact of strategic measurement, we first needed to define more clearly what we mean by "doing a good job at measurement." Surely, measurement proficiency does not simply mean "measuring more things." For example, years ago we encountered an information technology department of a large financial organization that was in deep trouble. Customers were clamoring, systems were failing, communication within the department and with customers just wasn't happening. The department was ripe for outsourcing or a change in leadership.

When we began to question managers about the department's measurement system, we found managers were tracking no less than 150 separate performance measures. Only an IT department has the capability to indulge in that kind of excess! The result was a plethora of unfocused, misdirected activities. Every manager in the department had selected a completely different subset of measures that he or she was trying to optimize. No two managers had the same set of top priorities. Not one measure represented the viewpoint of customers. Measurement in this IT department had run amok.

Our experience with this IT group, and other organizations, made it clear to us that *good measurement* involves a qualitative component. Companies that were truly proficient at measurement weren't necessarily measuring the most things. They realized that knowing *what not* to measure was just as important as knowing what to measure. *The most successful companies we worked with zeroed in on measuring the right things.*

Several recent academic articles have supported this same conclusion. Kaplan and Norton,[2] for example, have argued convincingly that effective organizational measurement involves measuring key components of the strategy from four perspectives: *financial, internal-business-process, customer, and learning and growth.* These four areas constitute a "balanced scorecard." Kaplan and Norton maintain that each perspective is critical to the long-term strategic success of an organization and that, consequently, an organization needs to continuously monitor a limited set of desired outcomes and drivers in each of these four areas.

Based on our work over the years with successful business strategies in a broad spectrum of industries, we believe there is great value in modifying Norton and Kaplan's four perspectives to the six identified in Table 1–1. The number of virtual organizations has steadily increased the importance of alliance partners and suppliers to effective strategy implementation. Consequently, we have added a "partners/suppliers" category to our key performance measurement areas. In addition, the majority of our clients include change and adaptability goals in several of their strategic performance areas, such as those dealing with new products, new employee capabilities, and improved operations. Therefore, they do not see a benefit to having a separate change and adaptability category of measures.

Table 1–1: KEY PERFORMANCE MEASUREMENT PERSPECTIVES

• Market	Includes customers and potential customers—both intermediate and end users—and competitors
• Financial	Includes shareholders or other financial stakeholders in the business, such as regulators
• People	Includes employees and labor suppliers or subcontractors
• Operations	Includes high-level process drivers or outcomes and key technologies
• Environment	Includes stakeholders that impact the organization's performance, such as regulatory agencies, environmentalists, and communities in which the organization operates
• Partners/Suppliers	Includes suppliers of both labor and materials, and alliance or joint-venture partners

We have yet to find a business strategy that cannot be represented in its key elements by performance goals within these six areas. In essence, these six areas represent classes of processes and major stakeholders that an organization must manage in order to be successful.

For us, measuring the "right things" entails measuring results in the six performance areas that are key to strategic success. And when we use the term "strategic measurement," we mean measurement focused on these six perspectives or areas of performance.

In identifying these six performance areas, we do not mean to imply that a company should devote equal attention to each performance area, nor that every company must measure all six areas. Different business strategies place different emphasis on managing—and therefore measuring—different areas. For example, the strategy of a refinery or chemical manufacturer is more likely to focus on operational and environmental issues than is the strategy of a retail organization, such as Sears, Roebuck and Co., which is likely to put greater strategic emphasis on measures of customer service satisfaction and employee commitment.

Rather, effective measurement-managed companies reach beyond financial performance to measure a combination of outcomes within most of the six performance areas. Precisely what they measure in each area will reflect their particular strategy for achieving long-term goals. Non measurement-managed organizations measure performance in fewer performance areas. What they measure is less closely linked to the business strategy than is the case with measurement-managed enterprises, and often reflects the absence of a well-developed business strategy.

While measurement has become the latest management hurrah, we were curious and wanted to know whether or not the increasing interest and new practices were indeed having an impact on business performance. We conducted an initial study in which we asked over two hundred senior executives in different organizations across the country what it was they were measuring and how measurement related to their business performance and cultures. Our aim was to determine whether "measurement-managed companies" in our study—those that tended to use a balanced set of measures across the six performance areas—performed better than their non measurement-managed counterparts.

To help in interpreting the survey results, we also conducted in-depth interviews with senior executives. These companies represented a variety of industries and ranged in size from Sears, Roebuck and Co. ($50 billion in sales) to Multiplex Co. ($27 million in sales).

From the survey respondents, we identified fifty-eight companies that employed measurement in a disciplined fashion. The executives of each of these measurement-managed organizations reported, first, that their strategy contained measurable objectives and, second, that they updated and reviewed *at least semiannually* measures in three or more of the six strategic measurement areas. We were able to compare these fifty-eight companies to sixty-four non measurement-managed organizations where executives reported that their company strategy did not include measurable objectives and that they updated and reviewed measures on a regular basis in only two or fewer of our six areas.

Once we had identified the two groups of contrasting organizations, we compared executives' ratings of their companies on three success criteria:

1. Whether or not their company was perceived as an industry leader over the past three years
2. Whether or not their company was financially in the top third of their industry group

3. How successful their organization had been in its most recent major change effort

Table 1–2 indicates that our measurement-managed companies—compared to their non-measurement counterparts—fared significantly better on all three success criteria.

Of the three success criteria, we were most struck by the superior performance of measurement-managed companies in implementing change efforts. Given the number of change efforts that are buried in the graveyards of so many competitors, it is notable that 97 percent of our measurement-managed companies report success with a major change effort. Even if we excuse this figure as overly self-congratulatory and lower the response value by 25 percent, the remaining figure would continue to be impressive. In studies of change we and a number of other investigators have undertaken, about 50 percent of the executives studied describe their efforts at major change as successful. Clearly, our measurement-managed organizations surpassed this figure.

Table 1–2: RELATING MEASUREMENT MANAGEMENT TO PERFORMANCE

Measure of Success	Measurement-Managed Organizations	Non Measurement-Managed Organizations
Perceived as an industry leader over the past 3 years*	74%	44%
Reported to be financially ranked in the top third of their industry*	83%	52%
Three-year return on investment (ROI)**	80%	45%
Last major cultural or operational change judged to be very or moderately successful*	97%	55%

*John H. Lingle and William A. Schiemann, "Is Measurement Worth It?," *Management Review,* March 1996, pp. 56–61
**Brian S. Morgan and William A. Schiemann, "Measuring People and Performance: Closing the Gaps," *Quality Progress,* January 1999, pp. 47–53.

One criticism we have sometimes heard of our initial investigation is that the financial performance data are based on self-reports by the interviewed executives, not hard financial numbers. Consequently, we undertook a subsequent study[3] in which we surveyed over eight hundred executives and examined financial performance both by self-report and by examining return on investment and return on assets from financial histories of the organizations. This second study found that the hard numbers corroborated executives' self-reports of financial performance and replicated the close relationship between financial leadership and sound measurement practices. More specifically, this study found that measurement-managed companies had a three-year ROI of 80 percent compared to 45 percent for non measurement-managed firms (Table 1–2).

MEASUREMENT-MANAGED ORGANIZATIONS: WHAT SETS THEM APART?

We spent a great deal of effort both in our quantitative research and in our hands-on consulting looking beyond the measurement factor to explain the difference between successful measurement-managed organizations and less successful non measurement-managed ones. No other significant factors emerged. Neither organizational size, industry type, nor number of employees involved in change could account for differences in market success between our measurement-managed and non measurement-managed companies. In addition, our second study also found that compared to other companies, industry financial leaders are:

- Far more likely to say they have a well-defined and balanced set of strategic measures and that such measures are used to help manage the business (69 percent vs. 39 percent)
- More likely than others to say that people measures are part of the balanced set of strategic measures (39 percent vs. 19 percent)
- More likely to have performance targets for non-financial people measures (42 percent vs. 20 percent), and more likely to hold people accountable for achieving these targets (44 percent vs. 22 percent)

Table 1–3: MEASUREMENT-MANAGED COMPANIES
EXHIBIT DIFFERENT CULTURES

Reported	Measurement-Managed Organizations	Non Measurement-Managed Organizations
Clear agreement on strategy among senior management	93%	37%
Good cooperation and teamwork among management	85%	38%
Unit performance measures are linked to strategic company measures	74%	16%
Information within the organization is shared openly and candidly	71%	30%
Effective communication of strategy to organization	60%	8%
Willingness by employees to take risks	52%	22%
Individual performance measures are linked to unit measures	52%	11%
High levels of self-monitoring of performance by employees	42%	16%

John H. Lingle and William A. Schiemann, "Is Measurement Worth It?," *Management Review,* March 1996, pp. 56–61.

When we looked more closely at the results of our first study of more than two hundred executives, we found other clear indicators of organizational success. Measurement-managed companies, compared to their non-measurement counterparts, displayed a number of cultural differences that are summarized in Table 1–3.

As you can see from Table 1–3, executives at measurement-managed companies report:

- Having a strategy that is better communicated to the organization (60 vs. 8 percent favorable ratings)
- More favorable levels of cooperation and teamwork among management (85 vs. 38 percent)
- Greater self-monitoring of performance by employees (42 vs. 16 percent)

- Employees who are more willing to take risks (52 vs. 22 percent)
- More open sharing of information (71 vs. 30 percent)

While culture can be difficult to quantify, measurement can play an important role in providing a common language for an organization to establish and monitor performance goals. For example, at Gilbarco, the $350 million manufacturer of gasoline-dispensing equipment, a "hierarchy of measures" is in place that cascades down from corporate headquarters. Said Thomas Rosetta, Gilbarco's manager of U.S. Operations, "Measurement provides clear, visible targets throughout the organization." It also gives the team-based environment at Gilbarco a "rallying point" for galvanizing group effort.

Thus, when we went beyond the financial performance data to how organizations operate on a day-to-day basis, a host of other differences between measurement-managed and non measurement-managed organizations surfaced. Based on our experience with a variety of measurement-managed organizations, we have summarized the most important differences in Table 1–4.

In contrasting attributes summarized in Table 1–4, it is important to emphasize that the differences between measurement-managed and non measurement-managed organizations transcend the number of things that are measured, or even what is measured. Rather, the distinctions reflect differences in the cultural fabrics of organizations and fundamental attitudes toward such things as what information should be shared, how decisions should be made, what effective leadership involves, and what types of behaviors get recognized and rewarded. As the book progresses, we will provide examples of how these differences in beliefs and values affect business performance. For now, we will highlight the differences by examining how an organization answers four important questions.

What Information Should Be Shared?

Executives at the best measurement-managed organizations share performance measures and information related to the measures to help them define and monitor business success. Sharing the responsibility for setting performance objectives and measures, along with information about how

Table 1–4: CONTRASTING ORGANIZATIONS

Measurement-Managed	Non Measurement-Managed
• Regular monitoring of a balanced set of performance measures that are linked closely to strategy implementation	• Heavy focus on financial measures, to the exclusion of most other types of measures
• Measures reflect a balance of long- and short-term goals	• Measures, when used, focus on the short term
• Open sharing of performance data across the organization	• Guarding and hoarding of performance data
• Review meetings primarily strategic in nature	• Review meetings often tactical in nature
• Organizational performance discussions take an integrated perspective	• Performance discussions tend to focus on a single symptom
• Measurement often used to help define concepts and clarify communication	• Communications tend to use many ill-defined terms
• Understanding and commitment to the strategy is high	• Understanding of the strategy is inconsistent across the organization
• Division, department, team, and individual performance measures tend to be linked	• Measures across the organization tend not to be linked or integrated
• Accountability and follow-through tend to be strong	• Many initiatives are begun; few seem to be effectively completed
• Employees are empowered and have access to whatever information is needed to make balanced decisions	• Bureaucratic decision processes continuously push decisions up the organization
• Employees see clear linkages between reward systems and achievement of strategic goals	• Performance management and reward systems send conflicting messages to employees concerning what is important

performance stacks up against these objectives and against best-in-class performance, often requires significant culture change.

A client of ours worked hard to become more measurement-managed. The company had agreed on a set of measures and performance targets that seemed to reflect its strategy. However, the measures were being ignored at quarterly review meetings. When we questioned the senior executive on why this was so, he responded:

> We do not have a tradition of airing dirty laundry in public. If there is a performance gap, people expect it to be raised one-on-one. The entire measurement effort is likely to be rejected if I start discussing performance gaps in public meetings.

Eventually, members of the leadership team began to review the measures at their meetings, discuss performance gaps, and share the relevant information in a group forum. Their initial resistance, however, illustrates the degree to which becoming measurement-managed can mean a change in the attitudes and beliefs of an organization.

How Should Decisions Be Made?

A great deal can be learned about the culture of an organization by watching an executive team make decisions. The best measurement-managed teams consider a range of pertinent information and review how a chosen course of action is likely to impact a multitude of performance areas. If revenues are not growing according to plan, the executive team will take a hard look at a range of possible influencing factors or "drivers." Do the customer measures suggest problems with customer satisfaction? Is a new competing product sapping market share? Are there morale issues with the sales force that are depressing performance? Is the training on new products progressing as planned?

Once a course of action has been identified, the best executive teams carefully review how a decision will impact other key areas of the business. "If we increase the hours of training, what additional time pressures will we place on the sales force? Will morale plummet even further by taking our sales people off-site? What might come off the plate to provide time for the training?" The best teams do an exceptional job at adopting an integrated perspective of the entire organizational system and their long-term strategic objectives when taking corrective action. The result is a course of action that produces both shorter- and longer-term success.

Contrast this behavior with less effective executive teams of non-management organizations that often engage in what we have labeled "data wars" and "decision jerk."[4]

Anyone who has ever attended a meeting knows about "data wars." It is the blood sport of executives who enjoy ambushing one another in meetings with data they have typically hoarded prior to the meeting. Data are used not so much as a means for making a reasoned decision but as a weapon to help advance a personal position. One symptom of a data war is the tendency of an executive team to spend more time arguing about the validity of the data than about the implications of a course of action. In such organizations, data are often collected and managed by a single department or individual, rather than discussed and planned for by the executive team prior to collection.

An organization plagued by "decision jerk" might meet to consider data from its employee survey and institute a program to address issues of employee morale. Two months later, when data from a customer satisfaction survey become available, a new program is launched to address issues of customer satisfaction. Then, two months after that, at budget time, financial cuts are suddenly introduced that place the employee and customer programs in jeopardy. The outcome is a series of stop-and-go, jerky initiatives that compromises management's credibility and leaves employees cynical about the organization's ability to follow through. A more integrated approach reviews the employee, customer, and financial data together and chooses a course of action that best addresses the priority issues raised in each performance area.

The best measurement-managed organizations we have known make decisions based on an integrated set of information that spans performance areas, rather than focusing on problems one event at a time.

What Does Effective Measurement-Managed Leadership Involve?

The leaders of measurement-managed companies typically view their role as one of helping others make decisions based on fact. They strive to establish a strategic framework, along with clear, measurable criteria that will allow others to make good decisions and move the organization forward. Such leaders use measurement to clarify the rules of the game. They know that once rules, objectives, and current performance levels are clear, employees know what they are responsible for and what they are authorized to do. Leaders in measurement-managed organizations give others access to a balanced set of performance measures that cover multiple strategic areas. This opens up employees' creativity and enables them to begin to think about the business with a more integrated perspective and evaluate their individual actions accordingly.

In contrast, in non measurement-managed organizations, employees are more likely to appear confused about objectives and success criteria. Under such circumstances employees are quick to pass decisions up the line. As a result, the role of leadership in non measurement-managed organizations often becomes more tactical than strategic in nature, as senior managers are drawn increasingly into day-to-day, operational decisions. Our experience is that in non measurement-managed organizations members of cross-functional teams are sent back to rework their recommendations much more often. Leaders too frequently send a disempowering message by redesigning the team's solution, or sending it back multiple times to "try again."

In contrast, in measurement-managed organizations the solutions that teams bring back to executives tend to be more strategic in nature and more consistent with thinking at the top. Measurement clarifies objectives and removes the fuzziness of success criteria, thereby allowing the leaders to gain a more strategic effort from employees.

What Types of Behaviors Get Recognized and Rewarded?

In both measurement-managed and non measurement-managed organizations, financial results are important. In either organization, managers who consistently miss their financial numbers are not likely to be rewarded.

However, in measurement-managed companies "hitting the financial numbers" alone is typically not enough. Rather, the organization has identified a clear set of capabilities or high-performance areas that must be accomplished first for financial success to be assured. We refer to these as "strategic drivers." They reflect the "how" component of the business strategy. Financial results are always important. But to be successful in the long run, an organization must improve its performance on these strategic drivers.

Table 1–5: THE HOW AND WHAT OF HIGH PERFORMANCE

| | | Drivers for Long-Term Strategic Goals | |
		Achieved	Missed
Financial Goals	**Achieved**	**Quadrant 1** Goals achieved, strategic drivers achieved	**Quadrant 2** Goals achieved, strategic drivers missed
	Missed	**Quadrant 3** Goals missed, strategic drivers achieved	**Quadrant 4** Goals missed, strategic drivers missed

Table 1–5 captures these two important dimensions. Because of their measurement system, measurement-managed companies are unlikely to be happy with managers operating in quadrant 2, even though the manager demonstrates an ability to achieve financial goals. Such organizations recognize that without managing the strategic drivers, the long-term success of the organization is in jeopardy. At the same time, measurement-managed companies are likely to show greater short-term tolerance of managers operating in quadrant 3, as long as failure to achieve financial goals does not represent operational deficiency but an investment in the future.

Measurement-managed companies are more concerned than their non measurement-managed counterparts about having leaders achieve success in a way that builds for the future, rather than achieving short-term success "at any cost."

WHY DOES IT WORK?

Measurement-managed organizations operate in a number of fundamentally different ways than their non measurement-managed counterparts. The outcome is superior financial performance, and sustainable results that enable organizations to excel over the long term. Why is this the case? The executives we talk with point to a number of reasons why they believe effective use of measurement is so powerful in enhancing their organization's performance.

Measurement Rapidly Forges Increased Strategic Agreement

In the absence of measurable objectives, we have learned not to assume that a senior management team agrees on the strategy. In a study that we published in *Across the Board* magazine, we found that nearly 40 percent of the executives we surveyed reported a lack of fundamental agreement on business strategy.[5] If we assume that not all senior executives were aware of disagreement within their own firm—or were, at least, unwilling to acknowledge such disagreement publicly—the real numbers may be far greater. And without agreement on the business strategy at the top, it is difficult to secure commitment, agree on resources, set priorities on major initiatives, or create integrated operational plans. Measurement helps remove the ambiguity and disagreement that surround high-level strategic concepts.

Measurement Provides a Common Language
to Communicate Strategy and Key Values

Understanding of the business strategy tends to dissipate rapidly as it filters down from the senior team. In surveys we have conducted in countless organizations, on average 40 percent of employees indicate they do not feel that they understand their company's strategy. The research we discussed previously shows measurement-managed companies do a better job at communicating their strategy. Measurement provides a precise language for describing the values or beliefs of an organization, what that organization wants to accomplish, and how it intends to accomplish it.

Measurement Helps Forge Alignment
Throughout the Organization

How can executives know if the actions of widely dispersed divisions and departments are supportive of the overall strategy? Maintaining alignment represents one of the greatest challenges for companies in today's rapidly changing business environment. The left side of Figure 1–1 illustrates the typical state of today's organization. Achieving perfect alignment is unrealistic. The arrow in Figure 1–1 illustrates the need to manage change continually. As the organization changes, some areas are aligned; others

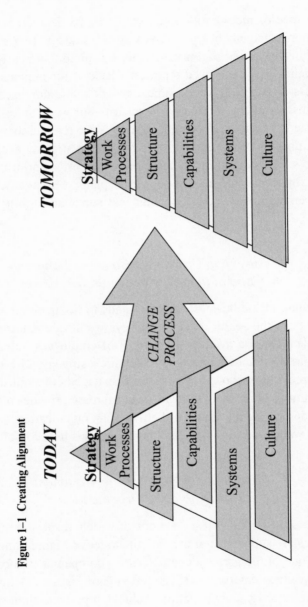

Figure 1-1 Creating Alignment

TODAY

Strategy

Work Processes

Structure

Capabilities

Systems

Culture

CHANGE PROCESS

TOMORROW

Strategy

Work Processes

Structure

Capabilities

Systems

Culture

are not. How can organizations know if they are properly aligned? One answer is strategic measurement. Having defined the important, critical few measures that indicate overall alignment, executives can more confidently manage market and workplace dynamics. How frequently must a measurement system be updated? As often as the business, the industry, and the strategy are changing.

In terms of alignment, executives tell us that measurement helps raise commitment to higher-level strategic objectives. As we shall see later on, the process of "cascading" measures throughout the organization helps make strategic objectives relevant to "my unit" and "my job." It puts business strategy close to the heads and hands of every employee.

Measurement Accelerates the Rate of Successful Change

Effective measurement provides an organization with unambiguous feedback on the progress of change. This not only improves the probability of success, but speeds the pace at which change occurs. A leading pharmaceutical organization with which we worked during a large merger serves as a case example. For a year during the merger, the company surveyed a sample of employees every month to assess their understanding of key communications, find out what work problems they were facing, and determine how well they understood the strategy of the new organization. The merger was accomplished in record time due to the company's ability to take action the minute problems began to surface. At one point, the entire agenda of a senior leadership meeting was changed at the eleventh hour in order to address a series of problems that had surfaced in the previous week's survey of employees. This type of rapid response helps a measurement-managed organization navigate the crosscurrents of change.

Measurement Increases a Company's Predictive Powers and Early Warning Capability

Strategic measures improve the ability of managers to anticipate future outcomes. This ability has been greatly facilitated by today's information technology. Senior executives are now able to set up an integrated relational database of key measures, allowing them to predict the effect of employee, supplier, and work flows on customer, market, and financial outcomes.

Studies by Ulrich, Wiley, and Schiemann[6] illustrate the vast array of employee measures that have been used effectively to predict important customer outcomes, such as customer satisfaction and retention, perceived product and service quality, share of wallet, and market share.

Work done recently at Sears, Roebuck and Co.[7] demonstrates a clear linkage among employee, customer, and financial measures. The company has identified a number of employee indices that predict customer defection and retail revenue. Sears, Roebuck's three strategic tenets—making the company a compelling place to shop, work, and invest—are all integrated with a network of strategic measures that provide early prediction of subsequent financial outcomes.

The interviews we conducted as part of our own research emphasized this tendency of measurement-managed companies to anticipate the future. In this regard, the advice of J. Walter Kisling, chairman and CEO of the Multiplex Co., a $27 million manufacturer of beverage dispensing equipment, is instructive: "Don't spend your energy measuring what you can't change. Spend your energy keeping up with and staying ahead of change."

Measurement Helps Provide Managers
with a Holistic Perspective

Effective measurement systems enable executives to take a comprehensive view of their entire landscape. With the integrated perspective strategic measurement provides, executives are positioned to see how actions taken in one area of the terrain can affect performance elsewhere.

For example, in one financial services company, the organization discovered the power of bringing together and making available to everyone information from the credit, collections, and account management functions. The organization has learned that a customer might leave based on gaps in any of these three functions and that a balanced combination of speed and accuracy is essential to high customer retention. Account managers want to extend more credit quickly, while credit officers want to ensure a capability to repay loans, and collectors must balance this with actions that can chase a customer away forever. Measures that span key performance areas help a management team consider and weigh the several critical forces that determine if the customer base will grow or shrink.

WHAT ABOUT THE FUTURE?

Our research indicates that measurement-managed organizations have enjoyed a competitive advantage in the past. We also believe strategic measurement will provide an even greater advantage for tomorrow's organization. Precisely why this is true is discussed in the next chapter.

CHAPTER 2

MEASUREMENT MANAGEMENT AND TOMORROW'S ORGANIZATION

M aking the investment to build a measurement-managed culture only makes sense if it will provide a competitive advantage tomorrow. Our research clearly points to the advantages measurement-managed organizations have today. But will these organizations continue to demonstrate the same performance advantages over their non measurement-managed counterparts?

We believe the future advantage will be even greater. To understand why, let us first examine the changing demands occurring in the business environment and understand how these demands are altering the management demands of organizations. The question we then must ask is: How valuable will a measurement-managed culture be to this future organization?

NEW CHALLENGES IN THE BUSINESS ENVIRONMENT

Let's face it, things have been changing dramatically. There is no need to rehash the change literature that dates back at least to Alvin Toffler's *Future Shock,* published in 1970. But it is instructive to focus on several key challenges that bear directly on the changing face of organizational management and the role that measurement might play in improving organizational performance. Figure 2–1 summarizes five challenges that are redefining the competitive environment and leading executives to develop new ways of managing their enterprises:

- Technology explosion
- Resource equalization
- Globalization
- Market sophistication
- New social values

Let's look briefly at each of these forces.

Technology Explosion

Technology is changing at warp speed and becoming smaller and increasingly portable. These changes are creating faster learning curves, more rapid access to best practices, and increasingly sophisticated competitive knowledge. Added to these is easier resource accessibility, with the result that the ability to replicate existing products and competencies has increased, while the probability of achieving a distinct product advantage for an appreciable length of time has decreased.

Figure 2–1 Five Key Challenges and their Implications

Resource Equalization

Over the past three decades, there has been a trend toward easier access to resources. Most firms can no longer exploit capital, new materials, labor, or information as platforms for long-term advantages. Capital markets are more robust than ever before, information is plentiful, and many raw materials have become commodities. It is difficult to gain a competitive advantage by easy access or control of a natural resource.

Globalization

Globalization continues to create greater access to new markets, labor, and resources. This and other forces have created a fundamental shift in supply and demand, leading to an abundance of suppliers competing for a growing but limited market. For example, India, not the United States, is one of the fastest-growing labor resource centers in the hunt for computer programmers. New offshore sources of skills like this offer cost advantages but pose a complex challenge of managing widely dispersed work forces with diverse cultural needs, expectations, and communication styles.

Market Sophistication

Education, technology, and the information explosion have produced much more sophisticated consumers, who are able more effectively to identify and compare a greater range and number of suppliers. These educated consumers demand better service, more innovative products, and competitive prices. Furthermore, customers are less interested in one-size-fits-all products. They want high-quality products customized to their unique needs. Increasingly, these products have a service component that must be delivered face-to-face. Consequently, products are produced "online" as opposed to in factories, and supervisors no longer have the luxury of conducting quality checks in centralized production facilities.

New Social Values

In a world of rapid change in which lifetime employment can no longer be guaranteed, companies are searching for new ways to instill a sense of commitment in their employees. For many, this means new work force values focused on increased ownership and opportunities for professional and personal growth. Many organizations are learning that they need to encourage greater employee participation in order to gain higher commitment, productivity, and innovation.

THE SEARCH FOR SUSTAINABLE COMPETITIVE ADVANTAGE

A quick glance at the five challenges and their implications conveys the dilemma facing most leaders today: There are few sustainable competitive advantages. No longer will a new product and patent provide future security for an organization.

The five challenges and their implications have created a new set of competitive advantages for tomorrow's organization. We have identified five of these in the right-hand column of Figure 2–2:

- An adaptive strategy
- Rapid, agile implementation
- Continuous innovation
- Mass customization
- An adaptive culture

An Adaptive Strategy

The challenges and their implications suggest that any competitive positioning based on products or technology is likely to be short-lived. As a result, an organization must position its basic strategic elements— mission, values, market scope and emphasis, and core competencies—to adjust rapidly to critical changes in the environment. That ability implies that the organization has a process in place for reviewing frequently the continuing efficacy of the strategy. This, in turn, implies more frequent review of the fundamental assumptions underlying a competitive position, such as competitor activities and trajectory, market analysis, core competency evaluation, and review of environmental forces. It also implies a willingness of the strategy team to update and change its strategy frequently.

Figure 2-2 Few Sustainable Competitive Advantages

Challenges	Implications	Potential Competitive Advantages
Technology explosion ◆ Information ◆ Miniaturization	◆ Better competitive knowledge ◆ Faster learning curves ◆ Rapid access to best practices	◆ **Adaptive strategy**
Resource equalization ◆ Capital ◆ Raw materials ◆ Information	◆ Limited product life ◆ Ability to replicate rapidly ◆ Time compression	◆ **Rapid, agile implementation**
Globalization	◆ Supply exceeds demand ◆ Access to broader idea pools ◆ Conflicting values, styles	◆ **Continual innovation**
Market sophistication ◆ Consumer education ◆ Growth	◆ Demand new/upgraded products ◆ Service expectations high	◆ **Mass customization**
New social values ◆ Work force ownership ◆ Growth	◆ Participation/involvement ◆ Mobility ◆ Learning	◆ **Adaptive culture**

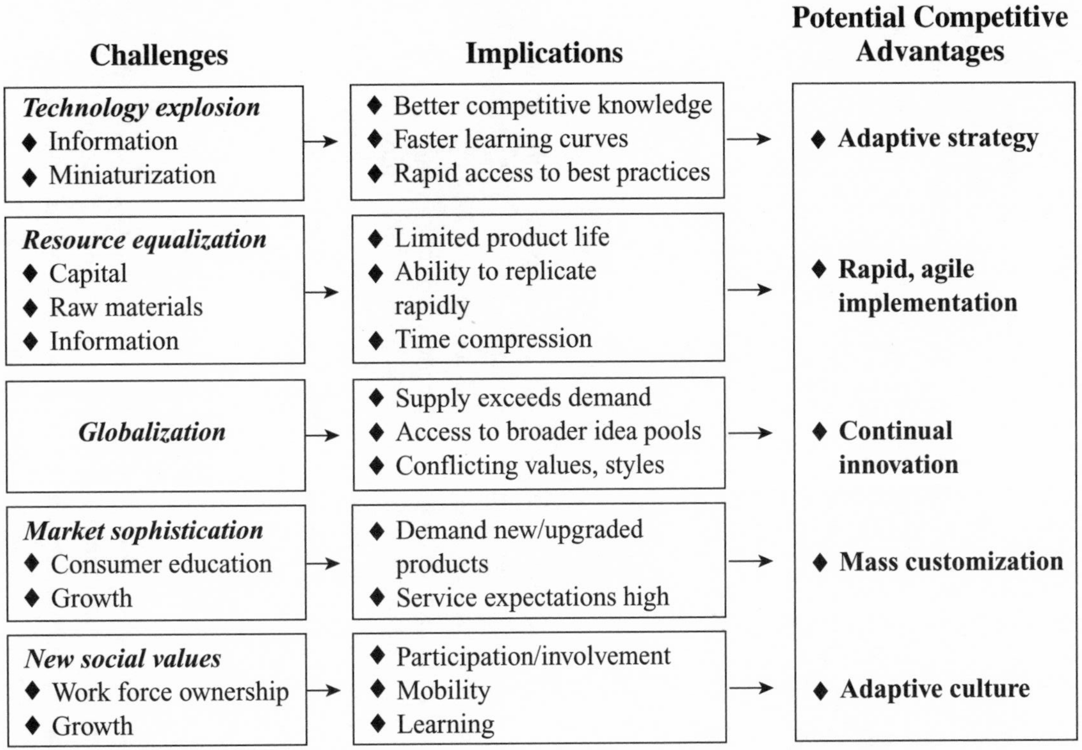

Rapid, Agile Implementation

In the "good old days," there was time to react to problems and plot their response. Take Xerox in the 1980s. Poor quality and savage attacks from more cost-conscious competitors brought Xerox to the brink. The company was able to reestablish its leadership position over six years by developing a quality culture. By 1997 Xerox's Return on Assets had grown to 18 percent (compared to 4 percent in 1984), productivity was up 117 percent, customer satisfaction was up 43 points, and Xerox stock had moved from $9 a share in 1990 to $88 a share in 1997.[1]

Compare this to the recent turnaround at Sears[2] or at Continental.[3] Each of these organizations achieved operational and financial turnarounds in less than forty-eight months. Today's CEOs do not have the luxury of time that Xerox had to improve their organizations' competitive profiles.

Continuous Innovation

A potential advantage for any organization is the ability to innovate continuously and faster than the competition. This has been the hallmark of such companies as 3M, Hewlett-Packard, and Disney. As we discussed, globalization forces create a larger idea pool from which to innovate.

New leaders, such as Robert Shapiro at Monsanto, are attempting to create new environments that truly foster innovation at increasingly accelerated rates. Monsanto has established a new and unique set of structures, systems, and values to drive creative competencies.

Mass Customization

Given greater customer education, sophistication, and information, there are increasing demands for new and upgraded products and enhanced services. Stan Davis introduced the concept of "mass customization" several years ago in his influential book, *Future Perfect*,[4] to help organizations understand that winning requires both the creation of highly customized products and services for customers, and the efficient use of the rapidly increasing arsenal of technology. Consider three quick examples:

- Today, Dell Computer will build a computer "your way," as the ad goes. In fact, that is the only way Dell will sell a computer. Building computers to order increases customer satisfaction, while at the same time significantly reducing Dell's inventory costs.
- For Christmas this year you can buy your child a doll that looks and dresses just like he or she does. Who wants a doll that looks like everyone elses, when you can have your very own "look-alike" offspring?
- And, in the area of "customized service," Amazon books keeps a profile of the books you have purchased from them and can automatically alert you by e-mail or a message on its web site when new books are published that match your profile of interests.

Effective mass customization requires an organization to have accurate information on the needs of different market segments, and an ability to make rapid changes to produce a variety of products and services efficiently.

Adaptive Culture

Having an adaptive culture may be one of the strongest points of differentiation. While organizations may not be able to control intellectual property, they can create a culture that embraces rather than resists change. In *Soul of a New Machine,* Tracy Kidder[5] described the culture of creativity that existed within a unique pocket of Data General. This enabled the company to surpass a formidable giant like Digital in introducing new technology. Others, like Heskett and Kotter,[6] have empirically demonstrated the tight link between performance and organizational cultures that are change friendly. Companies such as Hewlett-Packard, for example, eschew the cultural belief that an organization needs to avoid cannibalizing its own products. The result? A stunning 70 percent of HP's revenues come from products introduced in the last two years. The company has had a different lead product—calculators, personal computers, printers—in each of the past three decades.[7] The most successful companies of the future are likely to have strong, well-managed cultures that embrace change.

THE EMERGING KNOWLEDGE ORGANIZATION

New market challenges and the resulting requirements for sustaining competitive advantage doom to extinction traditional production organizations that have been prevalent for the past hundred years. As many have discussed before us, yesterday's production organization is being replaced by a radically different organization whose primary focus is the management of information, knowledge, and ideas in the service of speed, agility, mass customization, and a heightened change capability. In this new organization,

> The key to success is determined not by accident of possession, but by the capacity to generate new knowledge and the ability of the workplace to apply that knowledge skillfully in the production process. Thus, human resources—ideas, skills and knowledge—[have] replaced natural resources as a major source of production and wealth.[8]

Table 2–1 juxtaposes the traditional production firm with the emerging knowledge organization. The differences are dramatic and represent a fundamental shift in how we lead and manage our organizations. The knowledge organization has emerged as a highly interdependent, aligned set of structures, processes, systems, capabilities, and values that enable organizations to compete in the evolving world of unrelenting change.

The worst place for an organization to be is stuck somewhere in the middle—with one foot in the production organization and the other in the knowledge organization. Unfortunately, this is where many businesses seem to be. Executives in such organizations feel frustrated and bewildered when they become trapped in the quicksand of an isolated, never-ending series of interventions, change initiatives, and "renewal" programs that are intended to move the organization away from the old and into the new paradigm.

One fact is clear: Becoming a knowledge organization is a requirement, not an option. Everyone will migrate there sooner or later, or face extinction. The important question is, which organizations will realign themselves quickest to the new market realities? Management practices and systems that worked well within the old paradigm—for example, close supervision, limited span of control, hierarchical command and control, and heavy-handed management of financial and operational decisions—are ineffectual in the new knowledge organization of the twenty-first century.

In Table 2–1, where would you place your organization on each of the dimensions—in the left or right column? To the extent that your organization has a profile that includes characteristics from both the left and right columns, it displays a split personality that is likely to lower performance and confuse employees, customers, and other key stakeholders.

Table 2–1: TALE OF TWO ORGANIZATIONS

Twentieth-Century Production Organization	Twenty-First-Century Knowledge Organization
Marketplace	
Production driven	Market driven
• Production is king	• Customer is king
• Mass production	• Mass customization
• Relatively homogeneous consumer base	• Highly segmented, diverse consumer base
• Quality based on company standard	• Quality based on customer perceived value
Strategy	
Long-term strategies to reflect relatively stable business environment	Adaptive strategies to respond to dynamically changing business environment
• Geographically centralized	• Geographically dispersed
• Regional competition	• Global competition
• Big is better	• Adaptive is better
• Reasonable time to react	• Little time to react
Structure	
Hierarchical command and control structures	Flat, organic, low-control structures
• Many middle managers and supervisors	• Self-directed work teams
• Limited span of control	• Broad spans of control
• Function is supreme—silos	• Loosely-coupled cross-functional teams
• Functionally defined goals	• Functional, team, and individual goals linked across the organization

(continued)

Table 2–1 *(continued)*

Twentieth-Century Production Organization	Twenty-First-Century Knowledge Organization
Systems	
Managerially enabled	People and technology enabled
• Control by proximate supervisor	• Control by shared goals, values, and standards
• Data and information limited	• Rich information environments
• Managerially imposed strategy, tactics, behaviors	• Managerially driven strategy; employee-driven tactics, behaviors
• Limited authority, decision making	• Empowered work force
• "Need to know" communication	• Open communication environment
Capabilities	
Labor and materials focused	Knowledge focused
• Laborer work force	• Knowledge workers
• Materials, capital, and cost management preeminent	• Information, supplier, and people management preeminent
• Skills training for today's needs	• Knowledge building for tomorrow
Culture	
Narrow cultures	Adaptive cultures
• Ethnocentric	• Value diversity
• Commitment via command and intimidation	• Commitment via involvement, development
• Power from position	• Power from knowledge, skills
• Rewards for replication	• Rewards for innovation
• Risk avoidance	• Risk sharing

THE KNOWLEDGE ORGANIZATION AND MEASUREMENT MANAGEMENT

If the future belongs to the quick and nimble knowledge organization, what role might measurement management play? In Table 2–2, we juxtapose the major conclusions of Chapters 1 and 2. Across the top of the table are listed the requisite characteristics of the new knowledge organization that we have described in this chapter. Down the rows of the table are listed the six benefits of measurement management that we identified in Chapter 1. We have placed a check mark in each cell where we believe the knowledge organization will gain a key advantage from strategic measurement. The fit, as you can see, is remarkably strong.

Market Driven

In an environment in which the customer is king and product and services must be mass customized to a highly segmented and diverse customer base, a strategic measurement system is needed to track the dynamics of the marketplace. The early acquisition and utilization of knowledge allows an organization not only to react, but to anticipate likely changes in customer needs and expectations, competitor actions, and other market activities that influence strategy. Measurement helps an organization quickly see the need for change and then realign the organization behind new customer requirements.

Adaptive Strategies

Defining objectives in measurable terms provides a powerful tool to get senior leadership to common ground quickly—a critical advantage in forging new strategies for a dynamically changing business environment. It also forces management to take a more holistic view of the organization. The view down the mountain can become foggy without the benefit of measures across multiple areas to provide a sense of how actions in one area will impact other areas of the strategy. To effectively plot strategic change, an executive team needs clear and early feedback on where the current strategy is—and is not—working.

Flat, Organic, Low-Control Structures

In the face of widening spans of control, more independent teams, and challenging service requirements, a strategic measurement system provides a common language to link diverse groups together. This includes communication of goals, values, and work standards, as well as performance feedback to realign units that are out of sync or working at cross-purposes. The measurement systems can also provide an integrated view of how diverse groups are supporting the overall mission and strategy.

Table 2–2: BENEFITS OF MEASUREMENT MANAGEMENT FOR THE FUTURE KNOWLEDGE ORGANIZATION

	Market Driven	Adaptive Strategies	Flat, Low-Control Structures	People/Technology Enabled	Knowledge Focused	Adaptive Cultures
Rapidly forges strategic agreement	✓					✓
Uses a common language to communicate the mission, strategy, and key values of the organization		✓				
Helps forge alignment throughout the organization		✓	✓	✓	✓	✓
Accelerates the rate of successful change	✓✓	✓✓	✓	✓✓	✓✓	✓✓
Increases a company's predictive powers and early warning capability	✓		✓	✓✓		
Provides a holistic perspective					✓	

People and Technology-Enabled Systems

In the new rapidly changing service environment, individual and teams need to have timely information that enables them to set or challenge standards, take quick corrective action, and communicate quickly to other dependent groups. In this new information-rich environment, a strategic measurement system provides a tool to help create focus and set priorities, enabling rapid, front-line decision making.

Knowledge-Focused Capabilities

An effectively structured strategic measurement system provides feedback on core competencies, thereby enabling business units, functions, teams, and ultimately individuals to determine where they stand. With timely feedback on the development of critical competencies, the organization can determine where its largest gaps exist and how to allocate remedial resources effectively. At the unit level, integrated information from customers, suppliers, and other units allows rapid action to address knowledge and skill deficiencies.

Adaptive Cultures

Successful knowledge organizations will require strong but adaptive cultures that enable them to adjust rapidly to changing products, services, customer preferences, and the competitive environment. Amidst all the change, it will become increasingly critical for organizations to communicate clearly a central set of values that can serve as compass points of stability, yet be flexible enough to permit changes in areas demanding rapid adaptation. A strategic measurement system provides help in defining central values, in monitoring how well these values are being put into practice, and in assessing the degree to which internal and external change forces a reevaluation of those values. For example, we have seen Ortho-Clinical Diagnostics use measurement to help define a new set of values to serve as a template for day-to-day decision making, while preserving innovation and creativity in its demanding, fast-changing marketplace.

Figure 2–3 summarizes the linkage of strategic measurement to operating successfully in this new business context. Measurement management is pivotal for the knowledge organization and the sustainable results it implies.

Figure 2–3 New Challenges Require a New Approach

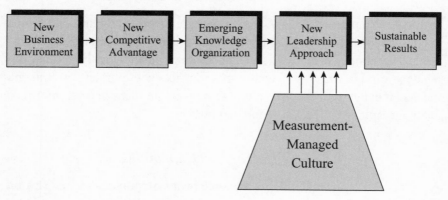

In Chapters 1 and 2 we have examined the first half of the measurement paradox: Is measurement worth it? We believe there is overwhelming evidence that it is. Today, measurement-managed organizations are performing better than their non measurement-managed counterparts. This measurement-based performance advantage seems certain to increase in tomorrow's knowledge organization. The next chapter looks at the second half of the measurement paradox. If measurement, now and in the future, provides such a strong competitive advantage, why aren't companies doing a better job at it?

CHAPTER 3

HOW WELL ARE
COMPANIES MEASURING?

Whenever we tout the value of measurement to senior executives and share the results of our research, we seldom receive an argument. We have yet to have an executive tell us that "Measurement is not that important," or "You can manage just fine without measuring," or "It's just not worth the effort to establish effective performance measures for your business." Furthermore, executives are flocking to conferences on strategic measurement in record numbers. The International Quality and Productivity Center reports that they have had over five thousand executives attend their workshops on strategic measurement in the last six years.

One could easily assume that with all the itinerant wisdom dispensed by the gurus, companies must be getting the message and doing at least a passable job at measuring what's important to their success. Don't bet the family farm on *that* assumption.

Over the past twenty-five years, we have conducted thousands of interviews with senior executives. What continues to surprise us is the hesitancy we frequently encounter when we ask questions such as: How do you assess the effectiveness of your human resources strategy? How do you know what value customers find in your products and services? How do you measure the organization's ability to change and adapt? There appears to be much greater hesitancy in answering questions like these compared to questions about revenue growth or profitability. Yet it is the answers to such questions that largely determine financial success.

Table 3–1: HOW EXECUTIVES VALUE AND TRUST AVAILABLE
INFORMATION

Measurement Performance Area	% of Executives Highly Valuing Information	% Willing to Bet Their Jobs on the Quality of Information
Market/Customer	85	29
Financial	82	61
Operations	79	41
People	67	16
Environment/Community	53	25
Adaptability	52	16

John H. Lingle and William A. Schiemann, "Is Measurement Worth It?" *Management Review,* March 1996, pp. 56–61.

Note: These measurement performance areas differ slightly from Table 1–1. The research in this chapter was conducted prior to our development of the current set of strategic categories.

Failure to raise the right questions—and answer them in a disciplined way—is partially a result of a lack of confidence in the information at the disposal of many executives. In our first study of 203 companies that looked at the advantage of measurement management, for example, we found that while most executives value and desire information in our six strategic performance areas, few are willing to bet their jobs on the quality of information available to them in these areas. Table 3–1 shows how executives rate the quality of available information versus their needs in our six strategic measurement areas.

While there is a moderately high level of comfort with financial measures, confidence in the other areas is dismal. For example, although 85 percent of the executives in our study view customer information as crucial to managing their business, only 29 percent report being confident in the quality of the information they have. In regard to people measures—measures of at organization's labor force such as competencies, commitment, and performance—only 16 percent of executives express confidence in their measures. And yet, how many of these executives would say, "People are our most important resource?" Lack of confidence in what is being measured pervades nonfinancial areas.

For most companies, people management is one of the most important elements of their strategic success. This is even more the case for the

Figure 3–1 People Measures: How Are Companies Doing?

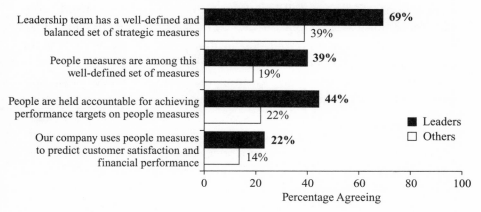

Industry leaders are ahead of the pack in people measurement, but they are not where they need to be

Leadership team has a well-defined and balanced set of strategic measures — 69% / 39%

People measures are among this well-defined set of measures — 39% / 19%

People are held accountable for achieving performance targets on people measures — 44% / 22%

Our company uses people measures to predict customer satisfaction and financial performance — 22% / 14%

Legend: ■ Leaders □ Others

X-axis: 0, 20, 40, 60, 80, 100 — Percentage Agreeing

emerging knowledge organization. And yet, again and again, "people" is a neglected measurement area.

In a study conducted in collaboration with *Quality Progress,* we asked eight hundred executives about the measures of employee commitment, satisfaction, and performance employed by their companies to help them manage their business.

We found that leaders—companies with higher Return on Assets and Return on Investments—were more likely to measure performance in such areas as culture, values, leadership, and employee commitment. For example, fewer than a third of the companies reporting that they use a "balanced set of strategic measures" say people measures are part of this set. Figure 3–1 summarizes the study's key findings showing that although industry leaders do better than non-leaders in measuring people, many of the leaders fall short of an effective people measurement process.

HOW STRATEGIC IS YOUR MEASUREMENT SYSTEM?

Our research and consulting experience has driven home to us again and again the fact that many companies are not doing a good job at measuring the things that have been proven to be important strategic drivers of business success. In this chapter we want to examine this issue more closely and identify the reasons why this is so. However, first we invite you to engage in a quick self-evaluation. Table 3–2 contains a brief quiz that has been abbreviated from a full measurement audit that we frequently conduct for senior leaders on the efficacy of their measurement system. Take a few minutes to test how your organization's Measurement Quotient, or M.Q., compares to our high performance norm.

How did you do? Are you measuring the things that matter to your organization's strategic success? Are you using these measures to help align and manage the organization? Or is your organization just another example of the measurement paradox? Based on the scoring instructions, if you are a "Measurement Star," you are among less than 5 percent of existing firms. If your system is "Medieval," you are not alone. Nearly 25 percent of enterprises we survey are in this category, but the number is dwindling as the proverbial "bar" is being raised. If your measurement system is either "Frontier" or "Pioneer," corrective action is needed.

WHY ARE SO FEW THINGS BEING MEASURED EFFECTIVELY?

Much of the remaining chapters of this book address the question, "How can an organization develop and implement an effective strategic measurement system?" To consider this question, however, we first need to understand better the causes of the measurement paradox. Why is it that so many executives have such little confidence in the information available to them in strategic measurement areas? And why don't they do a better job of measuring things in these areas?

Our research suggests part of the answer. Let's return for a moment to the finding we reported earlier that very few executives are willing to "bet their jobs" on the information available to them other than financial performance data (even though they are making exactly that bet on a daily basis!). We found two factors that contribute to this uncertainty: disagreement on what to measure and a failure to update information frequently.

Table 3–3 summarizes the answers we received when we asked executives to what extent measures of success were defined in their strategy for each of our six strategic areas, as well as how frequently their company updated measures in each area.

Table 3–2: HOW EFFECTIVE IS YOUR COMPANY'S MEASUREMENT SYSTEM?

I. QUALITY OF MEASUREMENT SYSTEM: The extent to which the strategic measures are good measures and the strategic measurement system is effective and reflects the long- and short-term goals of the organization. *(For each statement, circle the number which best describes your organization.)*

	Strongly Disagree	Disagree	Neutral	Agree	Strongly Agree
A. Our leadership team has 15–30 scorecard measures that they track to provide feedback on strategy implementation	1	2	3	4	5
B. It is possible to infer the *unique* qualities of my organization's strategy by looking at the strategy performance measures	1	2	3	4	5
C. There is strong agreement among the senior management team on *measurable* criteria for determining strategic success	1	2	3	4	5

II. BALANCE: The extent to which the coverage of the strategic measurement areas is adequate. *(For each statement, circle the number which best describes your organization.)*

	Strongly Disagree	Disagree	Neutral	Agree	Strongly Agree
A. The measures we track reflect a good balance between desired results and the organizational drivers of those results	1	2	3	4	5
B. The measures we track reflect a good balance between short- and long-term goals	1	2	3	4	5

C. Of the following strategic performance measurement areas, ***check*** those that you are using to drive broad organizational decision making.

1. Market/customers   _____

2. People (employees, contractors)   _____

3. Operations (technology, process, environmental)   _____

4. Environment   _____

5. Partners/suppliers   _____

6. Financial performance   _____

(continued)

Table 3–2 *(continued)*

III. CASCADING: The extent to which the process used to develop the strategic measures is effectively cascaded through the organization. *(Circle the most appropriate number for each statement.)*

	Strongly Disagree	Disagree	Neutral	Agree	Strongly Agree
A. The organizational strategy is well communicated and understood at all levels	1	2	3	4	5
B. Specific subunit targets have been set for each of the strategic measures of performance	1	2	3	4	5
C. Subunits feel ownership of the measures in each performance area	1	2	3	4	5
D. Each *department* has a balanced set of performance measures that are closely linked to strategic organizational performance measures	1	2	3	4	5
E. *Individual or team* performance measures are directly linked to unit and/or strategic organizational performance measures	1	2	3	4	5

IV. EMBEDDEDNESS: The extent to which the strategic measures are aligned with the performance and reward system in the organization. *(Circle the most appropriate number for each statement.)*

	Strongly Disagree	Disagree	Neutral	Agree	Strongly Agree
A. Strategic measures are linked to important rewards	1	2	3	4	5
B. Senior management holds itself accountable for improving performance in *all* strategic performance areas in their scorecard	1	2	3	4	5
C. All organizational units are held accountable for reviewing and improving their strategic performance measures on an ongoing basis	1	2	3	4	5
D. Individual and team competency development targets are linked to strategic scorecard measures	1	2	3	4	5
E. There is an easy-to-use information system that links scorecard measures across different organizational levels and functions.	1	2	3	4	5

Table 3–2 *(continued)*

V. CONTINUOUS LEARNING: The extent to which the strategic measures are continually evaluated and updated. *(Circle the most appropriate number for each statement.)*

	Strongly Disagree	Disagree	Neutral	Agree	Strongly Agree
A. Strategic performance measures are updated and reviewed at least semiannually	1	2	3	4	5
B. The organization continually evaluates and improves its strategic measures and the methods used to collect performance data	1	2	3	4	5
C. Senior management uses data from its strategic measurement system to evaluate and revise the way it manages the business	1	2	3	4	5

SCORING GUIDE

Section I:	Add up point value	total _____ (out of 15)
Section II:	a–b: add up point value	total _____ (out of 10)
	c: for each one checked add the	
	respective point value	total _____ C1: 3 points
		total _____ C2: 3 points
		total _____ C3: 1 point
		total _____ C4: 1 point
		total _____ C5: 1 points
		total _____ C6: 1 point
Section III:	add up point value	total _____ (out of 25)
Section IV:	add up point value	total _____ (out of 25)
Section V:	add up point value	total _____ (out of 15)

TOTAL SCORE: TOTAL _____ (out of 100)

80+ points: *Measurement Star.* Strategic measurement system is performing at a strong level. It is being used in an effective manner to move the organization forward.

60–79 points: *Frontier Measurement System.* Strategic measurement system is heading in the right direction; however, there are areas that would benefit from further improvement. It is important to look at the scores for each of the dimensions in order to better understand where changes need to be made.

40–59 points: *Pioneer Measurement System.* Strategic measurement system is performing at a minimal level of effectiveness. Some aspects of the system may be performing more strongly than others, but as a whole the system is in need of improvement. It is important to look at the scores for each of the dimensions in order to better understand where changes need to be made.

Less than 40 points: *Medieval Measurement System.* Strategic measurement is far behind in its effectiveness. Either the strategic measurement is in its early phases of development or aspects of the system are failing and need improvement. It is likely that improvement is needed for each of the dimensions.

The responses summarized in Table 3–3 reflect a pattern very similar to executives' confidence ratings. Apart from financial and operating efficiency, executives report that their success measures are neither clearly defined nor frequently updated in the other areas. Little wonder they feel uncomfortable betting their jobs on this information.

Most striking in these data is how few executives feel that their organizations have been able to define in clear, measurable terms what they hope to accomplish in the areas of employee performance, innovation/change, and community/environment. Even in the area of customer satisfaction, half the executives report disagreement within their company about measurable objectives.

Given a lack of agreement on what should be measured and the infrequent updating of the numbers, it is hardly surprising that most executives say they do not rely on this information to help them manage the business. This point is emphasized in Table 3–4, summarizing how executives report using information from different performance areas. As indicated, measures in areas outside of finance and operations are infrequently linked to compensation or used to help drive change in the organization.

Our research indicates that executives are not setting clear, measurable goals or updating measures frequently in areas other than finance and operations, nor are they using measures in these other areas to help manage the business. In effect, although executives may talk "measured results," in many areas they are not practicing what they preach. Once again, the all too familiar measurement paradox!

This analysis leaves unanswered the important question: "Why is it that more executives don't define—and update frequently—measurable objectives in areas like customer satisfaction, people performance, and innovation and change?" To understand the measurement paradox, we need to go a level deeper and identify the deterrents that impede or hinder executives from defining and measuring things outside of their comfort zone of finance and operations. If we understand these deterrents, we have a better chance of developing a successful process to overcome them and build more effective measurement-managed organizations.

Table 3–3: QUALITY OF MEASURES

			Performance Areas			
	Financial	Operating Efficiency	Customer Satisfaction	People Performance	Adaptability/ Innovation	Environment/ Community
Percentage of executives who believe measures are clearly defined in each area	92	68	48	17	13	25
Percentage of executives who report measures are updated and reviewed at least semiannually	88	69	48	27	23	23

Lingle and Schiemann, op. cit., p. 58

Table 3–4: USE OF MEASURES

			Performance Areas			
	Financial	**Operating Efficiency**	**Customer Satisfaction**	**People Performance**	**Adaptability/ Innovation**	**Environment/ Community**
Percentage reporting performance on measures in each area are included in regular management reviews	98	82	76	57	33	44
Percentage reporting performance on measures in each area are linked to compensation	94	54	37	20	12	6
Percentage reporting performance on measures in each area are used to help drive organizational change	80	62	48	29	23	9

Ibid., p. 59.

FIVE DETERRENTS TO BUILDING A MEASUREMENT-MANAGED ORGANIZATION

Over the years we have studied and worked with many different kinds of companies to improve their performance measurement systems. It has proven not to be a trivial undertaking, given the prevalence of five major deterrents that work against efforts to improve how an organization uses measurement. We believe that these five deterrents lie at the root of the measurement paradox and help explain why executives often talk a better game than they play when it comes to measurement. The forces are:

1. Fuzzy objectives, unclear definitions
2. Measurement miscues
3. Psychological resistance
4. Lack of leadership commitment
5. Cultural barriers

Throughout the rest of the book we will be discussing and providing examples of these deterrents at work, as well as proposing ways to limit their power to derail measurement improvement efforts. Let's discuss what we mean by each of them.

Fuzzy Objectives, Unclear Definitions

If you wish to debate with me, define your terms. Aristotle's advice is equally valid for managing—and measuring—organizations. The development of valid strategic measures requires that goals and objectives be defined with sufficient precision to be measurable. Typically, such precision exists in the financial and operational areas. Unfortunately, many companies do not invest the time required to define with equal precision desired performance in other areas, such as customer satisfaction, employee performance or innovation and change.

A first step in achieving precision in hard-to-quantify areas is to translate "soft" objectives into clear statements of results and then ask, "How can this result be measured?" For example, Ara Hovnanian, the leader of a highly successful home-building business, converts his company's guiding principles into specific "pledges" to customers, employees, and stakeholders and then attaches measurement criteria to each pledge.

Second, measurement requires that you specify behaviors implied by inherently imprecise terms such as "values," "culture," and the like. This allows managers to measure where they hit or miss the mark. For example, at Sears, Roebuck a good deal of attention and time has been paid recently to defining the company's values in behavioral terms. Only after this initial step is completed is it possible to set up a measurement system to determine where there is real progress.

Ask yourself how many hours your leadership team has spent discussing behavioral definitions of what you want to achieve in the areas of employee morale, values, innovation, and change as compared to financial outcomes, capital flows, and operational efficiencies? Not many, if your leadership team is typical. Unfortunately, the lack of definition around the first set of issues will make their effective measurement very difficult, if not impossible.

During a recent conversation with the authors, the president of a Fortune 100 manufacturing company confided that a number of people issues kept him awake at night. One of us then asked: "What information do you use to assess progress on these people issues? Do you have any measures or success criteria?" After thinking for a moment, the president responded that his organization periodically conducted employee surveys. When asked what the survey information showed about his areas of concern, he laughed, saying: "The last survey was three years ago. Everything has changed since that time." Then in a flash of enlightenment, he said, "I guess that's the point, isn't it?"

This leader lacked clear behavioral definitions of what was required from his work force. In the face of imprecise definitions and objectives, little concern was given to updating measures of work force morale and performance. The president went on to acknowledge that beyond six months, data decayed and could not be trusted. We asked him how often he measured the financials. He smiled. "Daily, weekly, monthly, depending on the report." Unfortunately, in the area that was causing him greatest anxiety—people issues—he lacked both precisely defined objectives and measurable success criteria.

As is often the case, members of this company's senior team participated in the process of formulating the strategy without really being in agreement. They had reached consensus on broad statements of strategic intent. It was easy at the 40,000-foot level to get everyone to nod in agreement over such pieties as: "Create greater flexibility in the work force"; "Achieve high levels of motivation and commitment"; and "Develop superior work force competencies." Who could argue with these generalities? Disagreement surfaces once you put a group to the test by asking it to define the success criteria for each statement. This type of precision is necessary as a first step to developing appropriate measures. Its absence represents a formidable barrier to improvements in a measurement system.

If you want to improve your measurement system, begin by defining more clearly the various components of your strategy-particularly in the nonfinancial and nonoperational performance areas!

Measurement Miscues

While accounting standards delivered by numbers crunchers predate the Middle Ages, measures of technology, customers, employees, suppliers, shareholders, and adaptability are more recent concepts with which executives are less familiar. Unfamiliarity breeds caution. Resistance to new measures in many cases appears to rest on a foundation of ignorance and misinformation.

To illustrate our point, Table 3–5 presents four statements about measures other than financial and operations. Which do you believe to be true? Executives, in expressing their opposition to "soft" or "nonfinancial" measures, often voice opinions like those in the table. In fact, the evidence

Table 3–5: WHICH OF THE FOLLOWING STATEMENTS ABOUT MEASUREMENT ARE TRUE?

1. Responses on employee surveys are typically influenced by how the business is doing at the time they are administered.
2. While helpful in planning product or service improvements, customer surveys are seldom accurate predictors of changes in market share.
3. It is always preferable to use "hard" measures rather than "soft" perceptual or survey measures.
4. Surveying customers or employees puts ideas in their heads and creates dissatisfaction.

indicates that none of these statements is true. Let's examine each a little more closely.

Responses on Employee Surveys Are Typically Influenced by How the Business Is Doing at the Time They Are Administered. While it is true that layoffs and downsizing can have a major impact on employee response to survey questions, the typical year-to-year business fluctuations, even when they affect bonuses and salary increases, do not. Many of the common items on a survey questionnaire reflect deeply embedded cultural attributes that are very enduring. For example:

"I am involved in decisions that affect my work."

"There is good cooperation and teamwork between departments."

"I understand the business strategy."

"My department works in a way that encourages the discovery of new and innovative practices."

For decades, we have distributed surveys with questions like these within the same organization and found little or no change in the percentage of employees responding favorably. Employee perceptions—and survey ratings—of basic cultural issues like these are extremely stable and difficult to change. Much more typically we encounter frustration among managers at how difficult it is to improve the numbers. With well-selected questions, and a good sample plan, survey data can be just as stable as traditional "hard" financial measures—and equally as difficult to improve without an effective action plan!

While Helpful in Planning Product or Service Improvements, Customer Surveys are Seldom Accurate Predictors of Changes in Market Share. If this statement had substituted the term "customer satisfaction" for "customer," it would have contained an element of truth. A number of organizations, such as Mercedes-Benz after the arrival of Lexus, have found themselves losing significant market share even while their "customer satisfaction" ratings remain as high as ever. These types of experiences have led some to conclude that "customer satisfaction" is not a very useful measure for predicting future market success.

However, "satisfaction" is only one piece of the customer perception puzzle. As Bradley Gale[1] documents extensively in his well-researched book, the key customer measure is not satisfaction alone, but rather "perceived value," or the ratio between satisfaction and price compared to competitive alternatives. Gale documents the ability of AT&T, and others, to predict changes in market share months in advance by using this type of perceived value measure. In spite of such evidence, many executives continue to question the reliability and validity of customer perception measures. With the right approach, executives can have in hand a powerful predictor for anticipating changes in their market position.

It Is Always Preferable to Use "Hard" Measures Rather Than "Soft" Perceptual or Survey Measures. A myth exists that a "hard" measure such as "percent turnover" is always better than a softer measure like a survey. Executives sometimes use this argument to resist conducting surveys of employees or of customers. Without discounting the value of hard measures, there are situations where survey measures can be both more economical and better predictors of business success.

Turnover is a good example. In most situations, by the time an organization begins to experience increased levels of voluntary turnover, something is seriously wrong. Typically, employees register a drop in morale long before they begin heading for the door. Survey measures can be an economical way to identify changes in loyalty and commitment long before an exodus begins. Identifying a problem early usually results in a less expensive solution. Because changes in perceptions typically precede changes in actions, measures that tap into the perceptions of employees or customers are almost always the best leading indicators of change.

The most effective measurement systems have a blend of "hard" measures and survey or other perceptual measures. The perceptual measures are typically the most sensitive leading indicators of change, while the hard measures serve to make sure the actions guided by the perceptions are ultimately successful.

Surveying Customers or Employees Puts Ideas in Their Heads and Creates Dissatisfaction. If you believe this statement, we would ask why it is that we have consistently found in our research that industry leaders, as compared to industry laggards, do more surveying of their customers and employees?

Table 3-6: WHY YOU NEED TO MEASURE COMPLAINTS

Customers who have a complaint worth $100+ ...	What % will repurchase or refer?
Who say nothing to the company	9
Who complain and the company...	
• does not resolve it	19
• resolves it	54
• resolves it quickly	82

Source: Direct Selling Education Foundation

In fact, evidence suggests that "not asking" is a much more dangerous strategy than "asking." Research reported by the Direct Selling Education Foundation[2] indicates that the average business never hears from 96 percent of its dissatisfied customers. For every complaint received, the average business has another 26 customers with problems from whom it has not heard. Table 3–6 summarizes what happens to these dissatisfied customers, depending on whether or not they are contacted. The value of eliciting complaints is clear. Simply allowing a customer to voice a complaint significantly increases the likelihood of repeat business. If the complaint can be dealt with quickly, eight out of ten customers will come back or refer others to your business.

"Asking" doesn't create problems. It provides an opportunity to address issues that can increase customer and employee loyalty.

There is one way in which "asking" does put ideas in people's heads. If you ask people about a subject, they are likely to conclude that you think it is important and that you are willing to address gaps or issues in this particular area. In this regard, "asking" is a powerful communication tool that expresses what an executive team believes is important. The lesson is not, "don't ask," but be sure you are asking about things that you are actually willing to address.

PSYCHOLOGICAL RESISTANCE

Both authors have graduate training in psychology and in quantitative methods. Working with companies to improve their measurement system often seems to draw more on our psychology training than our measurement training. There exist strong psychological barriers to changing a measurement system that contribute to the measurement paradox. These points of psychological resistance often reside in the leadership team itself. Why should this be the case?

First, success in the traditional production organization often went to the individuals with high needs for control. Second, many executives are driven to be successful. They want to win, however the "game" is played. These two traits are often directly challenged by a new measurement system that calls for different behaviors, challenges old assumptions, alters some of the rules of the game, or changes the information executives receive about how the game is progressing. When the rules and information are changed, executives become cautious, and may even bury data that may challenge their thinking. They want to make sure that they are as successful under the new rules as they have been under the old ones.

An example illustrates the point. One of the authors had been working with a company involved in a large merger. The company had been doing an excellent job of measuring employee perceptions on a monthly basis throughout the integration of the two organizations. Unfortunately, the data showed significant drops in employee morale. Worse yet, these low levels of morale persisted, in spite of a number of top-management initiatives designed to address some of the most salient problems. In short order, the executive team began to feel helpless, a feeling that was reinforced each month when the employee survey data arrived. The team's ultimate response was instructive. During one late-afternoon session the executives decided that the integration was complete and that they no longer needed to measure employee perceptions so frequently. In short, their response to losing control was, "If you can't fix it, stop measuring it." In this way they would no longer have to be reminded of their failings each month.

Psychological resistance to changes in the measurement system can be even stronger when existing measures are linked to executive pay. During our work with one large financial organization, the board had insisted that some percentage of executive compensation be linked to a measure of how well certain cultural values were being instilled in the organization. The demand was met with skepticism by most of the senior executives and many months were spent fine-tuning a survey instrument that focused on organizational values. During a meeting with the president, held after the survey had initially been administered, we were instructed to establish relatively low improvement targets for the next round of surveying. These targets had a 90 percent probability of being successful. Since the board-mandated measures could not be dismissed, the executives decided to focus their energies on controlling the situation by manipulating the targets. Payment of the bonus would be highly probable even with very limited improvement.

Established organizational systems are well entrenched and difficult to change. Employees, particularly in the executive ranks, strongly resist new and unfamiliar ways of defining success. They want to see the measures "work" for a while before they are willing to tie their future to them. Such resistance has defeated more than one attempt to improve management through measurement. Organizations often underestimate what is required to develop a sound set of measures and then share them in a way that builds buy-in and acceptance.

LACK OF LEADERSHIP COMMITMENT

No single factor is more important to an organization's ability to establish effective measurement practices than leadership. An example illustrates this point.

One of the authors worked with an organization that had been struggling to become more measurement-managed. The top executive team had spent significant time developing a limited set of high-level strategic measures. In addition, they had asked each of the five divisions to develop its own set of strategic performance measures linked to the high-level measures.

But there were problems. First, only half of the divisions responded and developed a set of strategic measures. Second, the organization's top leader was replaced. During several months of transition, the measurement effort was all but forgotten.

The new president, however, was a strong proponent of measurement. Early on, he held a facilitated one-day off-site meeting of all the division heads to review the strategy and associated measures. At the meeting, he declared that whenever he visited a division, the first thing he wanted to do was review the division's scorecard. Not surprisingly, the measurement effort was given new energy and attention.

This president not only preached measurement, he practiced it. It takes forceful, committed leadership to move organizational mountains, especially when one mountain is measurement.

CULTURAL BARRIERS

Anthropologists tell us that culture is a set of collective beliefs and behaviors that have evolved through shared experiences. Within organizational settings, these beliefs and behaviors are carried forward by folklore and stories about "the best" way to do things. Who has not heard someone say, "We don't do it that way here!"? Underlying such a statement is an implied set of norms or expected behaviors regarding organizational life that are subscribed to by members of that organization. These norms provide a communications shorthand for what "should" be done, and an implicit set of guidelines for decision making.

For most of us, cultural norms have become part of the tissue of daily routine. They do not need to be revisited or confronted. Commenting on this point, Edgar Schein[3] has observed that many of the underlying assumptions of a culture have become unknowable at a surface level. The story was told about a woman who always cut off the ends of the ham before she baked it. "Why do you do that?" the woman's six-year-old daughter asked. "My mother taught me to do it. It helps the cooking," was the response. In fact, the woman's mother started the tradition simply because she did not have a pan large enough for baking the ham, and so she cut the ham to fit the pan she had!

Organizations likewise have approached measurement based on tradition and accepted ways of doing things. These traditions, or embedded cultural norms, are formidable barriers to change. Many organizations are still cutting off the ends of the ham, even though it may no longer make sense to do so.

One particularly insidious cultural belief held by many organizations is an unjustified trust in informal feedback systems, such as complaints and criticisms about products and services from the sales force. While informal channels can provide an idea of the range of issues an organization faces, they do not provide accurate information on the extent of the problem. Such "incidence documentation" often leads to a few squeaky wheels getting attention, while a more critical problem goes unattended.

Or, take the question of who should have access to information in an organization. "Rules of Information Access" are built up over years of operation and typically reflect the management style of the senior-most organizational leaders. They not only determine who is allowed to see information, but affect the capability of different levels of management to use information effectively. Simply deciding to share information with more people does not solve this capability problem. For example, sharing Economic Value Added (EVA) figures or employee survey results with a new group of managers serves little purpose if the managers don't know how to interpret the information effectively or use the information to make better business decisions.

Many efforts to improve an organization's measurement system run squarely up against the five deterrents to change. However powerful these forces may be, they can be overcome by a more strategic approach to measurement. The next chapter describes such an approach.

CHAPTER 4

LEVERS FOR A MEASUREMENT-MANAGED ORGANIZATION

B ased on our experience over the past several decades, we have identified four key leverage points for building a measurement-managed organization and culture. When managed effectively, these four leverage points can be powerful platforms for helping organizations make the transition to a measurement-managed culture. These leverage points are:

1. Development of a transformational leadership model embedded in a fact-driven philosophy
2. Institutionalization of a new type of measurement system
3. Alignment of an organization's infrastructure to support the strategy and measurement system
4. Focus on behaviors

Let's look at each briefly.

DEVELOPMENT OF A TRANSFORMATIONAL LEADERSHIP MODEL

Managing today's fast-paced organization with strategic measurement requires a different, transformational approach to leading, similar to what Terry Anderson has defined as ". . . vision, planning, communication, and creative action that has a positive unifying effect on a group of people around a set of clear values and beliefs, to accomplish a clear set of measurable goals."[1] Table 4–1 highlights some of the differences between older leadership styles and this new approach.

Unfortunately, today's managers are often not prepared to assume the mantle of the new leadership requirements. As Howard Fisher from the Wharton School of Business puts it:

> There's an inconsistency in the process of becoming a top manager and being a top manager. A developing manager focuses hardest on "managing" better—bringing together technical disciplines such as manufacturing, marketing, selling, and financing. The premium in top management, though, is less on "managing" and more on leading—supplying vision, providing inspiration, and influencing action. The development process short-changes the role of leadership. . . . [B]eing a successful top manager means overcoming the limitations of becoming one.[2]

Many of these new leadership behaviors are essential to creating a measurement-managed organization.

One such behavior relates to how information flows through an organization and how it gets used. In traditional organizations, information

Table 4–1: LEADERSHIP STYLES ASSOCIATED WITH
THE MEASUREMENT-MANAGED ORGANIZATION

Measurement-Managed	Non Measurement-Managed
• Market driven	• Internally driven
• Decisions made where knowledge is	• Decisions reside at top
• Control the strategic; delegate operational	• Control everything
• Rapid decisions	• Slow, careful decisions
• Share knowledge	• Hoard information
• Optimize entire system	• Optimize functions
• Team success; joint risk	• Individual stardom
• Use judgment	• Follow rules
• Listen	• Tell
• Predict market, financial outcomes	• Evaluate market, financial outcomes

lumbers through formal structures far too slowly and in too fragmented a way for decision making in the new time-sensitive, competitive environment. Those who can share information directly between critical decision points will have a major competitive advantage over those who must filter, synthesize, and weigh this information the traditional way. The implication here is that leadership involves an openness to sharing information, and, on some issues, letting others take primary responsibility for managerial information. This is likely to be a shock to those who grew up believing that information is power. Ultimately, it is not the information that will create power in the future, but the ability to facilitate and move it. Leaders who can facilitate information flow will be the most successful in a measurement-managed organization.

Transformational leadership also requires a move toward shared decision making. Organizations are more complex today, requiring a good deal of information gleaned from many sources. Customers have become more sophisticated and demanding. Employees often work asynchronously and at great distance from one another. Workers want more opportunities to grow and learn. Leaders who can let go yet maintain good decision-making skills will enjoy the advantages of speed and flawless execution in the marketplace.

A third major shift in behavior for the new leaders is the change from individual stardom to group success. Traditional organizations tend to favor the superman approach to leadership. In today's fast-moving, highly complex, interconnected world, the focus is less on teams than on constantly shifting clusters of individuals and groups, with different clusters becoming more or less important depending on the issue and on the intellectual capital required to resolve the issue. Increasingly, strategic success measures tend to reflect group, rather than individual accomplishments. This places a greater management focus on group success and joint risk taking.

Whatever an organization's approach to strengthening its measurement system, it must start at the top of the organization with a modified set of leadership behaviors. Without a new kind of leadership, it is impossible to overcome the deterrents arrayed against effective measurement system change and evolution. Clarifying the strategy, confronting psychological resistance points among managers, and breaking down embedded cultural responses simply will not happen without leadership.

A New Type of
Measurement System

The next leverage point for making the transition to a measurement-managed organization is building a different type of measurement system. Table 4–2 contrasts the measurement systems of today's effective measurement-managed organization with more traditional measurement systems. Traditionally, in many organizations information was controlled and used as a stick rather than a carrot. Executives learned to create it as functional specialists and then evolved it as a weapon to control resources and fight whatever "data war" was raging.

Another feature of most measurement systems of the past was the singular focus on financial results. Much of this information was cloaked in arcane complexity and secrecy, making it virtually impossible for others to understand it and participate in changing it.

The new measurement system calls for increased participation in understanding and using information throughout the organization. Individuals and teams at every level are expected to understand how related teams are doing, the results each team is achieving, and the respective roles of various teams. In addition, there is a greater focus on predictive measures that enable users to anticipate likely outcomes, in the hope that being forewarned allows everyone to be forearmed. The measurement system becomes more of a "pull" than a "push" mechanism for influencing and controlling the organization. In other words, teams seek out performance feedback on a continuous basis, rather than having feedback forced on them by a higher-level supervisor.

In the more traditional organization, measurement serves as a monitoring device primarily used to "take the temperature" of the organization and help supervisors know where to focus their attention. In the measurement-managed organization, measurement fulfills three different functions that lie at heart of how the organization operates on a day-to-day basis:

- Links strategic ideas to behaviors
- Integrates performance across the organization
- Provides a mechanism to increase self-accountability

Let's briefly look at each of these.

Table 4–2: CHARACTERISTICS OF THE NEW MEASUREMENT
SYSTEMS

Traditional Measurement System	New Measurement System
• Used for control and power	• Used for knowledge
• Centralized	• Decentralized
• Used to audit imposed account-abilities	• Used as feedback for self-assumed accountability
• Accessed on "need-to-know basis"	• Open access to information
• Financial/operational information dominates	• Balanced stakeholder information
• Results measures dominate	• Balance of predictive and results measures
• Information is functionally driven, resides in silos	• Holistic information is linked across functions, stakeholders, processes

Link Strategic Ideas to Behaviors

In many traditional organizations there is a wide gap between strategic objectives and behaviors. For example, while strategic discussions focus on such things as capital deployment, market penetration, and product differentiation, employees in the trenches are addressing expenses, production rates, safety, and cycle time. The links between the strategy and front-line behaviors are fuzzy at best to most employees, including executives.

This contrasts with the measurement-managed organization in which there is a clear line of sight between strategic themes, strategic measures, and individual behaviors. If penetration of a new market is a key element of the strategy, the route by which this penetration will occur is carefully specified, key behaviors are identified and measured. For example, assume the strategy involved introducing a new product by a segment of the sales force that is targeted to a particular customer segment. Measures would be developed to track key elements: the speed of product introduction, the quality of sales force training on the new product, the number of targeted customers contacted, the percentage of revenue being generated from sales of the new product. The measures are defined and communicated so everyone knows how well the implementation of the strategy is progressing. The measures serve as a roadmap to link specific behavior back to the higher-level strategic concepts.

Link Performance Across the Organization

When there is a need to make rapid changes to elements of the business strategy, a balanced strategic measurement system can quickly adjust, providing a linking mechanism across the organization to help keep the organization aligned and on track. A holistic measurement system helps employees in different units to understand how their actions influence other parts of the organization and enables them to react to developing changes in other areas.

A subsidiary of a major energy company recently discovered that its traditional market niche was collapsing, creating dramatic new pricing pressure. It used a strategic scorecard to help realign everyone behind a set of new initiatives designed to overcome the situation.

Because the measurement system was closely linked with the performance and reward system, the organization was able to gain everyone's attention when it introduced several new measures that allowed subunits to evaluate immediately the impact of their actions on newly introduced cost and efficiency goals.

Beyond the vertical linkage that enabled subunits to realign their measures and behaviors in support of the new direction, the measurement system also brought an increased level of cross-functional thinking to the organization. Functions began to increase their communication with one another as they came to realize the degree to which the actions of other regions and divisions were influencing their ability to optimize performance on the new measures.

Increase Levels of Self-Accountability

In the traditional production organization employees tended to work in close proximity to a supervisor who monitored the performance of a small number of employees, holding them accountable for imposed production goals. In the new knowledge organization, work forces are more dispersed, and spans of control are wider. Services are manufactured "on-line," face-to-face with the customer. It becomes difficult for a supervisor to monitor the day-to-day performance of individual employees. Clear objectives and the measurement system become mechanisms for employees to monitor performance and hold themselves accountable for established standards. Recall our research showing that executives in measurement-managed companies report that their employees are both more creative and more accountable for their own actions compared to non measurement-managed organizations. Self-accountability is a key element of the new measurement-managed culture, and is aided by a good measurement system that provides rapid, relevant feedback.

AN ALIGNED INFRASTRUCTURE

Our third key leverage point for developing a measurement-managed organization is aligning the organizational infrastructure to support it. By infrastructure, we mean the key business processes, organizational structure, systems, competencies, and culture of the organization. What we mean by alignment is simply the degree to which each of each of these infrastructure elements supports the business strategy.

If it is to have lasting power, it is also important that the infrastructure of an organization support the same goals and objectives that the measurement system supports. If the business strategy and its related measurement system focus employees' attention on, say, financial, customer, and people measures, the reward system should encourage performance in all three areas. If it does not, over time the measurement system is likely to be ignored and will lose its power to influence behavior.

In Chapter 8 we will discuss in some detail alignment issues that are most critical to supporting a new measurement system. Foremost among these are:

1. Management decision systems—for example, budgeting and resource allocation
2. Human resource systems—for example, performance management, rewards, training, and selection
3. Information technology systems—for example, management information systems and intra-company communication systems
4. Continuous improvement systems—for example, annual planning, and product development systems

The experience of a large service organization illustrates the importance of these elements. The organization had spent a year developing and refining a high-level strategic scorecard, and by everyone's account, the effort had been successful. Senior executives felt there was a common understanding and commitment to the strategy. The measurement system was up and running, and helped refine the strategy in several areas where thinking previously had been fuzzy and incomplete.

Yet, there were problems. Performance in several key strategic areas had not improved at the hoped-for rate. In many departments employees continued to complain of inconsistent leadership and poor understanding of the strategy. The work force did not appear to be fully committed and accountable for improving the numbers. In some departments employees ignored the new measurement system entirely.

As they cast about for an explanation for the lack of enthusiastic acceptance of the measurement effort, the leadership team discovered that the individual performance planning system remained completely divorced from the scorecard effort. Managers continued to meet with employees, but the discussions and goal-setting conversations never connected to the higher-level scorecard measures.

To correct the problem, the company set out to redesign the individual performance planning system. This included new planning worksheets that incorporated aspects of the scorecard and extensive manager training on ways of linking individual goals to the strategic measures. At the end of the second year of the new planning system, the company was able to hit several aggressive stretch targets. In addition, the company's employee survey for that year showed significant improvements of 15 to 25 percentage points on questions related to employees' understanding of the strategy and key organizational goals. While measurement began the improvement process, only when other organizational systems were aligned with the new measurement system did the company realize its potential.

START BY CHANGING BEHAVIOR

A final leverage point that underlies much of our approach to helping organizations improve their measurement system is to focus first on behavior change, with the assumption that attitude change follows behavior change.

Years of work in various organizational settings has convinced us that attitudes are not changed by memos, CEO speeches, or "rah rah" from supervisors. In fact, recent research questions whether the attitudes that underlie organizational culture can ever be changed through rational dialogue. David Kearns, the former CEO of Xerox, who turned around a company at the edge of an economic precipice, certainly found this to be the case. He tried many different "rational" avenues to changing behavior, only to meet with great resistance. His senior executives denied much of the real data regarding the company's position; they had effectively created walls around the organization that protected their view of reality. Preaching and verbal warnings were not effective roads to attitude change.

As another example of how difficult it is to change entrenched attitudes even in the face of hard evidence, Ford managers and workers resisted change even as Honda and other Japanese competitors began gobbling up market share. Ford found it hard to believe that its premier position could be threatened in spite of mounting evidence. The organization's values and ways of operating had worked in the past and, presumably, would work again in the future. Even when executives and workers at Ford realized that there were gaps between their operating values and new business realities, it was not easy to change attitudes or reinvent the culture. People fell back on old approaches, hoping that "this too shall pass."

A large body of psychological research supports the conclusion that it is difficult to change strong attitudes through persuasion. This is perhaps most clearly illustrated by research findings that changes in attitude typically correlate much *less* with the persuasive arguments a person remembers than they do with the internal thoughts generated by that person at the time the persuasive arguments are heard![3] Again, intuitively we know this to be the case. If you want to know whether or not you changed my attitude about something, don't ask me if I understood and remembered your arguments. Rather, ask me what I thought about your arguments when I heard them. My internally generated thoughts or feelings in response to your arguments are the most important influences on any possible change in my attitude.

The fact that changes in attitude follow changes in behavior has been demonstrated in literally hundreds of psychological studies. As early as 1959, two researchers, Festinger and Carlsmith,[4] showed that attitudes tend to change in order to be more consistent with people's behaviors. Others[5] have demonstrated that people actually experience negative feelings when they hold attitudes that are inconsistent with the way they behave. The stronger these uncomfortable feelings, the more likely a person is to change attitudes in a way that makes them more consistent with the behavior.

Following these research findings, many learning programs are built on the premise that we must initially find ways to encourage employees to experiment with a new set of behaviors. If employees find that these behaviors serve them well, they will not only repeat them, but will also begin to change their attitudes. In essence, we are reversing Edgar Schein's process of how culture changes.[6] It is "unformed" by getting people to experiment with new behaviors, to receive new information, and to expose them to situations that challenge old assumptions. If the new behavior can be sustained, attitude changes are likely to follow.

The same principles hold true for changing cultural attitudes in organizations. Individuals—leaders and employees alike—need to be able to experiment with new behaviors in order to reassess and change their attitudes. Organizations that go through this process collectively begin to change their cultures because the successful new behaviors lead to changes in attitude which, when reinforced, lead to new behavior norms and values.

Our approach to changing attitudes about measurement follows similar steps. It starts with an attempt to motivate new behaviors, but not by preaching. Our counsel is to provide inducements to experiment with new behaviors related to good measurement practices in a nonthreatening environment with quick benefits that will reinforce and encourage a repetition of the new behaviors. This simple, but powerful, model is represented in Figure 4–1.

The first box on the left of Figure 4–1 suggests that individuals are more likely to look at alternatives when they have doubts or discomfort with their existing behaviors or attitudes, as was the case at Xerox. The next box reflects the notion that some inducement must be provided to engage members of the organization in behaviors that will be consistent with the desired attitudes that underlie a measurement-managed culture. These behaviors then need to be reinforced quickly to increase the probability that they will continue. Finally, if the behaviors continue with positive outcomes, changes in attitude, represented by the final box, will occur. This, in turn, encourages the repetition and elaboration of the behaviors, shown by the return arrow back to "new behaviors." Incidentally, research has consistently shown that new behaviors that are induced with minimum force are likely to lead to the greatest amount of attitude change.[7]

Figure 4–1 Attitude Change Model

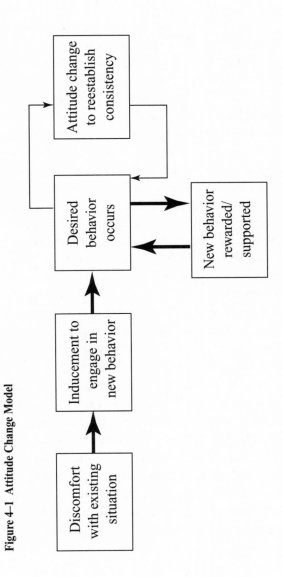

The quality movement is a good overall example of successful organizational change that was driven with behavioral modification rather than rational persuasion. The first requirement of change in our model—dissatisfaction with the status quo—was certainly occurring among U.S. manufacturers as record numbers of Americans were buying Japanese products and choosing their suppliers more selectively. Everyone, managers and employers alike, was beginning to feel the pain but few were changing in any strategic way. Then, quality circles were initiated as a way to engage employees in new behaviors. The first quality circles were crude, but contained several essential ingredients, most notably experimentation with new behaviors in a nonthreatening environment—the second requirement of change in our model. They provided a new way to examine data, make decisions, and influence outcomes. Beyond providing inducements to getting people to participate in teams, many were given financial payouts for ideas and solutions, recognition from senior managers, and awards for essentially behaving differently. These inducements or benefits—the third requirement in our model—helped to reinforce new team behaviors while teams were in their infancy, and this, in turn, created experiences around a new way of working that began to have payoffs.

Once Xerox, an early adapter of this approach to quality, began to produce higher-value products to customers at lower cost, working to improve quality continuously became *the* way to behave. And, after several years of these new behaviors, the attitudes became closely aligned with the new way of doing things. Xerox employees would defend, explain, and proselytize the values of this approach and for good reason: It worked.

This simple, effective model has guided our work in helping organizations to establish a measurement-managed culture. Typically, we begin to apply this model with senior leaders, and continue to use it with employees at every level as measurement-managed activities are cascaded throughout the organization. The culture-change process we describe in the remaining chapters relies heavily on this approach.

CONCLUDING THOUGHTS

There are a number of forces that resist development of more effective measurement systems in organizations. These forces tend to lead to the measurement paradox discussed earlier in the book in which favorable statements about measurement, and proven bottom-line results do not lead many companies to adopt the measurement-managed framework. Successful implementation of a measurement-managed organization requires an effective cultural change process that we describe in the remainder of the book. That process pivots off the four leverage points we have discussed, and has helped many organizations across the industrial landscape overcome the barriers we have identified to achieve major culture change in how they employ measurement.

Your organization may not be ready for large-scale change. If this is true, read on nevertheless. There are big gains to be made by taking small, incremental steps toward improving measurement within your organization. Our approach is designed to provide early positive outcomes at each step.

PART II

BUILDING THE MEASUREMENT-MANAGED ORGANIZATION

S everal years ago, while working with a large manufacturer to develop a cultural assessment survey, one of the authors ventured to ask an executive from the company whether his organization had developed a strategic scorecard. His response showed deep frustration:

> If you are talking about developing a balanced scorecard, don't mention that term around here. We must have spent several million dollars trying to design and implement a scorecard with little success. Scorecard is pretty much a dirty word at this company.

While this company's sizable financial investment in scorecarding was fairly unusual, the difficulty that the organization had encountered was not. Our best guess is that approximately 50 percent of those organizations setting out to implement major changes in their measurement system feel the effort was less than fully successful. Not surprisingly, this 50 percent unsuccessful rate matches closely the failure rate typically reported for major organizational change efforts such as reengineering and total quality management.

As we discuss in Chapter 1, truly successful measurement-managed companies do much more than build a simple "scorecard" of measures. Becoming "measurement managed" means changing leadership practices, information sharing patterns, and forms of accountability. In short, it typically represents a broad set of cultural changes that challenge the way in which information is used, shared, and managed. How can this change occur? What steps can be taken to lessen the 50 percent failure rate for major organizational change efforts?

Successful implementation of a measurement-managed culture requires the successful completion of four broad phases. Each phase contains several key requirements, or gates, that must be navigated in order to complete that phase successfully. Understanding the nature of these gates, and how to navigate them, is key to evaluating a measurement system. The majority of measurement system failures we encounter result from the inability to successfully navigate one or more gates in the process.

While a major cultural transformation may require years to complete, benefits from the journey can—*indeed must*—come much faster. If new behaviors are not quickly and directly reinforced with benefits, old behaviors will rapidly reassert themselves.

To illustrate the successful navigation of the four phases, chapters 5 through 8 will share the story of an organization that has transformed itself into a measurement-managed enterprise. While our narrative focuses on one company, we will add our experiences from other organizations to round out the story. The actions and experience of our case organization illustrate in a concrete fashion an approach to the culture change process that has proven successful in a wide variety of organizations.

"Only the fool learns from his own mistakes," Otto von Bismarck once stated, "the wise man learns from the mistakes of others." In this spirit, we also report on some less successful efforts to help illustrate ways in which ineffective processes and actions have thwarted change.

Figure II–1 summarizes the four phases involved in establishing a measurement-managed culture. Beneath each phase is a series of challenges that must be met or "gates" to navigate to successfully complete the phase. Before examining Phase I in detail, let's briefly review all four phases to see how their successful navigation can help an organization overcome some of the barriers we identified in the previous chapter.

Figure II–1 The Four Phases for Developing a Measurement-Managed Culture

I. Define	II. Design	III. Cascade	IV. Embed
Gates:	*Gates:*	*Gates:*	*Gates:*
1. Clear process objectives formulated	1. "Theory of the business" tested	1. "Cascading" structure determined	1. Management process integrated
2. Agreement on strategy secured	2. Valid reliable measures identified	2. Strategy communicated	2. HR systems aligned
3. The "theory of the business" defined	3. Performance targets set	3. "Cascade" leaders trained	3. IT system linked
4. Top leadership commitment secured	4. Process leaders developed	4. System of measures linked	4. "Theory of the business" refined
		5. Measurement behavior linked	

Phase I: Defining the Strategy

When we first began working with organizations to improve their measurement systems, we didn't fully appreciate that debates about measurement can begin too early. Without a solid foundation in strategy, discussions about measurement quickly become unfocused. Worse, a premature discussion of measures can gloss over executive disagreements about the business strategy and underlying differences about what really drives organizational success. Phase I involves building the required agreement among members of the executive team that is a prerequisite for effective measurement. The final output of Phase I is agreement on a limited set of concepts that need to be measured and a well-elaborated rationale for why this is the case.

Phase II: Designing the Measures

In Phase I an organization defines *what* exact performance areas it must measure; in Phase II it decides *how* exactly to measure them. Here is where the myths and prejudices must be addressed concerning what can and cannot be measured. As suggested by the brief summary of the key gates (Figure II–1), in addition to designing technically correct measures, Phase II provides an opportunity to test and validate the "theory of the business," as well as the opportunity to build increased understanding and commitment to the measurement model.

Phase III: Cascading the Measures

The power of a measurement system is fully realized only when measured performance in strategic areas guides day-to-day decisions. For this to happen, the high-level, enterprise-wide strategic measures must be communicated throughout the organization. Managers must understand the strategy and receive regular performance updates. In addition, they need to extend the measurement system to their own departments, and eventually to each employee.

Phase IV: Embedding the Measurement System

To really take hold, other systems, processes and structures must support any major organizational change. So it is with a measurement system. Ultimately, employees act in ways that are consistent with the rewards they receive, their capabilities, the information that is accessible to them, and the values exhibited by senior leaders. Measurement systems begin with a tenuous hold on an organization. To survive and strengthen over time, a measurement system must be aligned with, and supported by, other systems and work processes in the organization. Like all other systems, measurement must be continually improved.

We are now ready to look more closely at Phase I and the gates connected with it.

CHAPTER 5

DEVELOPING THE
STRATEGIC TEMPLATE

In working with different organizations, we are often asked, "How can I know that we're measuring the right thing?" The short answer is that the strategy and "theory of the business" should tell you. A really good measurement system tells a clear story about the road an organization has chosen to compete successfully. Phase I is all about making sure "the story" is clear.

PHASE I: DEFINING THE STRATEGY—
GATES TO NAVIGATE

Phase I involves having the leaders develop precise process objectives, and clarify their strategy and "theory of the business" so that key results—and the drivers of these results—can be measured. There are four gates for successfully completing Phase I.

Gate 1. Clear Process Objectives Formulated

Objective setting can be especially difficult for a leadership team when the challenge is as nebulous and complex as "culture change." An important first step is to break the culture change effort into bite-sized chunks and set benefit-yielding objectives around each piece.

Figure 5–1 The Four Phases for Developing a Measurement-Managed Culture

I. Define	II. Design	III. Cascade	IV. Embed
Gates:	*Gates:*	*Gates:*	*Gates:*
1. Clear process objectives formulated	1. "Theory of the business" tested	1. "Cascading" structure determined	1. Management process integrated
2. Agreement on strategy secured	2. Valid reliable measures identified	2. Strategy communicated	2. HR systems aligned
3. The "theory of the business" defined	3. Performance targets set	3. "Cascade" leaders trained	3. IT systems linked
4. Top leadership commitment secured	4. Process leaders developed	4. System of measures linked	4. "Theory of the business" refined
		5. Measurement behavior linked	

With most executive groups, the process of clarifying objectives for culture change begins with education about what a measurement-managed culture entails, and what the journey to achieving it involves. Specificity in setting objectives is crucial. For example, one objective of the change process might be to have the senior executives work more effectively as a team. This, in turn, can be separated into smaller chunks, such as "ensure the top team's understanding of and commitment to the business strategy," and "improve the information flow and ways to provide feedback to team members."

One of the most important reasons for clear objectives is that without them, executives tend to be less willing to invest the needed time, energy, and financial resources required for success.

Gate 2. Agreement on Strategy Secured

In a study on change that we conducted several years ago, we found that 39 percent of executives interviewed reported that their company's last major change effort had failed because of a lack of top management agreement on their business strategy.[1] This finding parallels our experience in the field.

Too often, even when a written summary of the strategy exists, members of the senior team disagree on what the strategy means and how it can best be implemented. Without clear agreement on the strategy, it becomes difficult for a group of individuals to determine what is really important and what, therefore, needs to be measured.

Gate 3. The "Theory of the Business" Defined

Ask a roomful of executives what one major change will significantly improve their organization's performance and you can bet you will get many answers. One executive may favor increasing the "share of wallet" through improved service; another may well argue for increasing market penetration through rapid acquisition of new customers, perhaps through a strategic alliance; yet a third may advocate greater penetration of new markets with existing products through greater marketing investments and better account management. These arguments reflect different implicit theories or models that each executive team holds about the best way to increase the organization's success. Each alternative theory, in turn, includes assumptions about what needs to change first—service quality, development of alliance partnership, or account management capabilities.

Before deciding on what to measure, an executive must agree on what we will refer to as the "theory—or the model—of the business," those fundamental premises that form a framework for decision making and for determining which organizational improvements will most likely achieve the strategy. Any of the fundamental theories we just discussed could serve as a starting point. Each, of course, needs further elaboration. If the executive team decides that major growth will come through increased sales to existing accounts via better marketing and account management, the next question is: How can this best happen? Will new sales representatives need to be hired, or can improved sales training achieve the desired results? What is the effect on other organizational priorities and on current resource allocation?

The organization's broad strategy needs to be elaborated and translated into a model that represents the most critical organizational elements that must be carefully managed for success—both drivers and results. Later in this chapter we will present one such model, or theory, in discussing our case study.

Gate 4. Top Leadership Commitment Secured

A colleague of ours likes to talk about "passing the water-cooler test," or what an executive is likely to say about a decision during informal discussions around the water cooler. A comment like, "We decided to open the Northeast—what a dumb idea," represents a major failure of the test. To pass, an executive must communicate not only the content or decision, but also his or her support for it. When decisions by senior executives fail the water-cooler test, inconsistent, disparate messages at the top reverberate down through the organization, creating confusion and cynicism. To maximize the chances of change success, members of a leadership team must not only know the strategy, the theory of the business and the project plan, but they must be committed to them and be willing to communicate their unequivocal support.

How can the senior executive team navigate the four gates to successfully complete Phase I of the cultural change process? Let us turn to our case study for answers. The case places heavy emphasis on the behavioral requirements for senior leaders. Ineffective leader behaviors can diminish even the best change process.

SUCCESS AT FACTEX

Factex is a major financial services organization with approximately one thousand employees and a $20 billion loan portfolio.

When Factex's president first starting thinking about changing his company's culture, he was in an enviable position. Factex had long been a leader in its financial services niche, both in reputation and in profitability. The company's market performance was stellar, with two back-to-back years of record earnings.

But as the president looked into the future, he saw growth in his company's market niche becoming sluggish at best. He also saw new forces coming into play that were likely to shrink demand for his company's products in key customer groups. How would he be able to grow the business in this rapidly changing, threatening environment?

Surveying the internal capabilities of the organization, the president saw a number of serious problems. Factex was steeped in financial and managerial conservatism. It was hierarchical in structure and built on multiple fiefdoms. Functional leaders spent more time sparring with one another than cooperating to capture new clients. A recent employee survey highlighted many of these problems. A high percentage of employees rated the company low on teamwork and cooperation, innovation and risk taking, clarity of strategy, decision making and communications effectiveness.

To add to this challenge, the company had recently purchased a major rival of almost equal size. The technical systems—as well as the cultures of the two organizations—clashed at numerous points, reinforcing employees' sense of confusion, conflicting priorities, and lack of teamwork.

In short, although the company had been successful, the president knew the organization was ill prepared to meet the looming challenges it faced. Without faster growth, spurred by entry into new markets, the company was almost certain to fail.

To meet these challenges the president began to search for a mechanism to refocus the organization on new markets and unleash what he believed to be the latent creativity of a very competent but risk-adverse work force. He knew he needed to engage the thinking power of every employee, to enhance his or her skills and create an environment where knowledge flowed up, down, and throughout the organization. While he did not realize it initially, this president had begun the journey toward measurement management.

Different organizations move through the gates of Phase I in different ways. At Factex, the journey took just under two months. During this time, the authors worked closely with Factex's leadership team to guide the company through the four gates. This, in turn, entailed four sets of activities:

1. Educating the senior team about a measurement-managed organization in order to build support for the project
2. Dedicating time at several staff meetings to gain consensus around a set of clear process objectives
3. Securing agreement on the business strategy and making explicit executives' implicit theories of what would drive success for the organization operationally
4. Translating the strategy into a clear business model

While these four actions don't exactly parallel the four gates of Phase I—reality never matches the confines of a model—once Factex accomplished these activities, the top team successfully navigated our four gates.

Few journeys can be completed successfully without a guide. Factex's journey into measurement management was no exception. One of the most important actions taken early on was to appoint a senior-level manager as process guide for the effort. His responsibilities included:

- Monitoring the process and raising warning flags if things got off track
- Maintaining close communication with the leadership team to encourage its continual enthusiasm and support for the implementation effort
- Educating and coaching executives about their role in the process
- Anticipating roadblocks and working with the "process facilitator" to successfully circumvent them
- Scheduling interviews and meetings

Such activities can consume between 25 and 50 percent of a process guide's time.

The politically sensitive nature of the process guide's role requires that he or she possess special personal characteristics. The process guide must have the respect of members of the leadership team and be able to gain their attention. The guide must also be politically astute, be able to assume a strategic perspective, be comfortable with numbers, have superb process skills, and possess a solid understanding of the business.

The president of Factex appointed a vice president who had worked closely with the senior team for several years to be the process guide. Several external consultants served as process facilitators, supporting the vice president. This internal-external team worked together to keep the process on track.

With the process guide in place, let's turn to the specific steps taken by Factex to steer successfully through the gates of Phase 1.

Step 1. Educating Executives and Building Support for the Project

The successful change project needs more than supporters at the top. It also needs champions. Given all the change and churn in an organization, a new initiative must fight its way onto the crowded agenda of the leadership team.

The "champion building" process at Factex began with the president. He had read about the scorecard concept and attended several executive briefings on the subject. In search of something to drive cultural change in his organization, the president thought the scorecard might be the answer. To be successful, however, he knew he would have to rally the support of other members of the executive leadership team.

In early discussion with the president, we encouraged him in his efforts to build support before launching the project. We argued that developing champions involved progressing along the continuum illustrated in Figure 5–2, from becoming aware to becoming knowledgeable, to becoming a supporter, and finally to becoming a champion.

At the awareness stage, an executive first becomes conscious of the change process and the benefits it offers. In Factex's case, understanding what a "measurement-managed" culture really entailed took further education. Only a knowledgeable person can become an effective supporter or champion, since a person who is simply "aware" has no ammunition to convince a doubting Thomas, or to help stay the course if the winds of support shift direction.

The need for knowledge requires ways of repeatedly exposing executives to the details of the process and its benefits. This may involve encouraging attendance at conferences, making presentations at board meetings, and taking time during interviews and discussions with executives to "sell" the process.

Knowledgeable executives may become supporters, but they will not necessarily be champions. The difference between a supporter and a champion is somewhat analogous to the distinction between managing and leading. A manager does the expected, encourages participation, and helps make sure the mechanics of a process remain on track. A leader, on the other hand, develops and communicates a vision that encourages others to sacrifice individual self-interest for a larger cause.

Figure 5–2 Steps to Building Champions

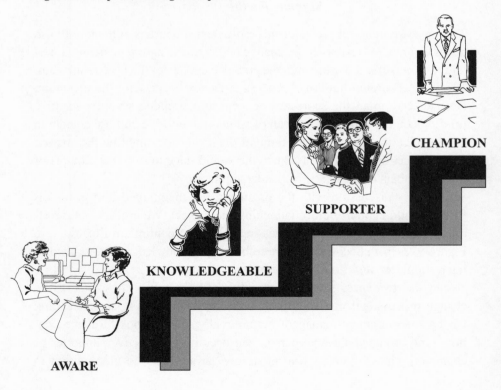

So it is with the champion, as opposed to a supporter. Supporters go along with the process, and may even encourage others to do the same. A champion anticipates problems others do not see and proactively takes steps to keep the process on track and in line with a larger vision. A champion actively recruits others to the cause, as opposed to guiding those who are already on board. Some of the differences between a champion and a leader are summarized in Table 5–1.

At Factex, the president took an active role in building supporters and champions. He invited several knowledgeable speakers to make presentations on strategic measurement at staff meetings. In addition, the president convinced his senior team to join him at a national conference on strategic measurement at which team members could talk with other executives who were involved in similar efforts.

In many cases, organizations will begin the process with just a few champions. In some cases, the president may not be a champion. Other executives may step forward and push the process initially. As the process unfolds, it is important to continue the champion-building process through education and the highlighting of benefits that derive from each step of the journey. The small cadre of initial leaders needs to be expanded as the process expands.

Table 5–1: ACTIONS OF A CHAMPION VERSUS A SUPPORTER

Actions of a Supporter	Actions of a Champion
Speaks in a supportive way of the process	Speaks inspirationally about the process
Helps maintain support for the process	Recruits new supporters for the process
Reacts to and helps smooth out problems that arrive in the process	Anticipates process problems and moves to address them before they occur
Avoids public actions that might appear not to support the process	Actively looks for public opportunities to support the process
Attends and participates in process activities	Generates and plans process activities

Step 2: Gaining Consensus Around
Clear Process Objectives

Many executives fail to set clear objectives for a process before launching it. Not at Factex. At a number of staff meetings, prime time was set aside for discussing this change effort. These discussions led to the following goals for the change process:

- Substantially accelerate growth of the company's revenues and profits
- Change the culture of the organization to be:
  - → More market focused, less inward looking
  - → More innovative, less bureaucratic
  - → More team oriented, fewer "silos"
- Increase employees' understanding of the strategy at every level
- Increase employees' accountability for results, not just activities
- Provide tracking systems that allow the organization to know earlier when problems occur in implementing the strategy

As part of developing the strategic scorecard, the top team agreed that measures were needed to track the achievement of the change process goals.

The top team also thought carefully about more specific goals for Phase I of the process. In order to successfully apply the change model, members of the leadership team knew that Phase I would need to begin changing a number of leader behaviors, as well as providing some quick benefits to encourage continued commitment to the process. With this in mind, the following objectives were established for Phase I:

- Engage the senior team in a way that would demonstrate some "quick-wins" from the measurement improvement efforts
- Identify and tackle areas of disagreement in interpretation of the strategy
- Develop a business model or "theory of the business" that linked the most important strategic goals with the causes or "drivers" of these goals
- Create a change plan for involving others in the task of designing and deploying the scorecard

Several points are of special importance in regard to the objective-setting process at Factex. First, these objectives were arrived at through education of and discussion with members of the senior team. Only after the leaders became committed to the objectives was it possible to discuss in a productive manner the process that might be used to achieve the objectives.

Second, resources and time commitments were obtained from Factex's top team because there was early recognition and articulation of the fact that the strategic measurement effort would be an ongoing process designed to change the management dynamics—and the culture. As one executive put it, scorecarding is an "ing," not a "thing." In other words, the scorecard itself would provide a limited set of measures, but this would be just the tip of the iceberg. More important was the submerged "process" by which the scorecard would be developed and deployed through the organization. This process—not simply the numbers—would be the vehicle for changing the way the organization was managed and run. Recognition of this larger objective encouraged senior executives to stay involved and not delegate the process to lower levels.

In thinking through the issue of change, the discussion invariably raises questions: How ambitious should the change effort be? And, what should be communicated about it? In some cases, the CEO or president may be seeking limited improvement. Communication to the senior team should reflect this intent. When the change is more ambitious, should senior executives be shielded from the magnitude of the effort? Given our experience with organizational change and measurement, we would, as a rule, say "no."

One danger of not discussing the objectives is that the senior team may feel deceived, or somehow "baited," as the effort unfolds and begins to grow in size. A second danger is that the process will slow down and lose momentum as time is spent selling the next steps at the end of each phase. Finally, the greatest danger is that the senior team will not feel compelled to assume a leadership role, since the process was never framed as one sufficiently important to require senior-executive commitment and leadership.

If one key objective is cultural change, we have found consistently that the best approach is to gain senior-executive commitment to the broader objectives up front. Once this is achieved, it is possible to create more limited objectives corresponding to each gate and deliver tangible benefits as each objective is achieved.

Clear, up-front objectives provided the Factex executives with a framework for evaluating progress and justifying the time and resources they were investing in the project. It is highly doubtful that the project could have achieved such success if a consensus on objectives had not been reached early on.

Step 3: Evaluating Agreement
on the Business Strategy

The president of Factex was not sure that his leadership held a common understanding of the strategy, despite the fact that less than a year earlier, many days had been spent developing a written strategic document. Since then, several members of the leadership team had changed and there were ongoing debates about key points in the strategy at several recent leadership team meetings.

Before tackling the measurement issue, we urged the Factex president to identify and reconcile difference in interpretation of the strategy. Although not fully convinced that a problem existed, the president agreed to a plan to assess the level of strategic agreement.

The evaluation plan consisted of having each executive complete a brief questionnaire and participate in a forty-five-minute, one-on-one interview about his or her interpretation of the strategy. Key discussion points included:

- Perceived strengths and weaknesses of the organization
- Competitive strengths and weaknesses
- The biggest growth opportunities in the marketplace
- Projected revenue mix three and four years out for the most important products, services, and customer segments
- Things that most needed to be changed in the organization
- Strategic goals
- Core competencies required for success
- Priority areas for action—what needed to be tackled first?

This evaluation revealed several strategic chasms within the leadership team. The president needed no more convincing. Before his organization could move forward, directional differences had to be resolved. The president called for a series of off-site meetings with the leadership team. Data collected during the evaluation was used as the baseline for the initial discussions.

For example, at Factex almost all of the executives saw a need to become increasingly automated in handling credit transactions. This point had been rigorously debated in the earlier strategy formulation sessions. Since everyone agreed this was a key to future success, there was no need to discuss it at length. There also was widespread agreement that future success required penetration of new industry sectors. But the question became how to achieve this goal. There were almost as many different ideas about how to penetrate new industry sectors as there were senior executives. This was clearly an area that demanded attention. The preparatory work made it possible to separate issues and focus attention to reach common ground.

Step 4: Translating the Strategy into a Clear Business Model

The final step taken to navigate the Phase I gates at Factex was to translate the business strategy to a clear theory or model of the business that identified how the organization planned to achieve the strategy. This was accomplished at an off-site meeting. By "model," we mean a picture that illustrates the links among strategic goals and the most important upstream drivers or success factors that enable the business to achieve these goals.

Two points are important in understanding this process. First, the leadership team at Factex was not "creating" a new strategy. This had been done earlier through a series of lengthy meetings and summarized into a written document. There was no need to reinvent the wheel.

Second, the team needed to extract from the strategy the most critical elements that they would manage as a group. An illustrative example of such a model is presented in Figure 5–3.

The ovals to the right of the model represent key results that Factex hopes to achieve as part of its strategy; the boxes represent crucial drivers of these results at which the organization must excel. The arrows represent links among the performance areas and results from the perspective of the senior team members. Improvements in the performance areas within each box tend to occur first, "driving" performance in the ovals to the right. For example, at Factex the leadership team felt that in order to

Figure 5–3 Factex's Strategic Model of Business Success

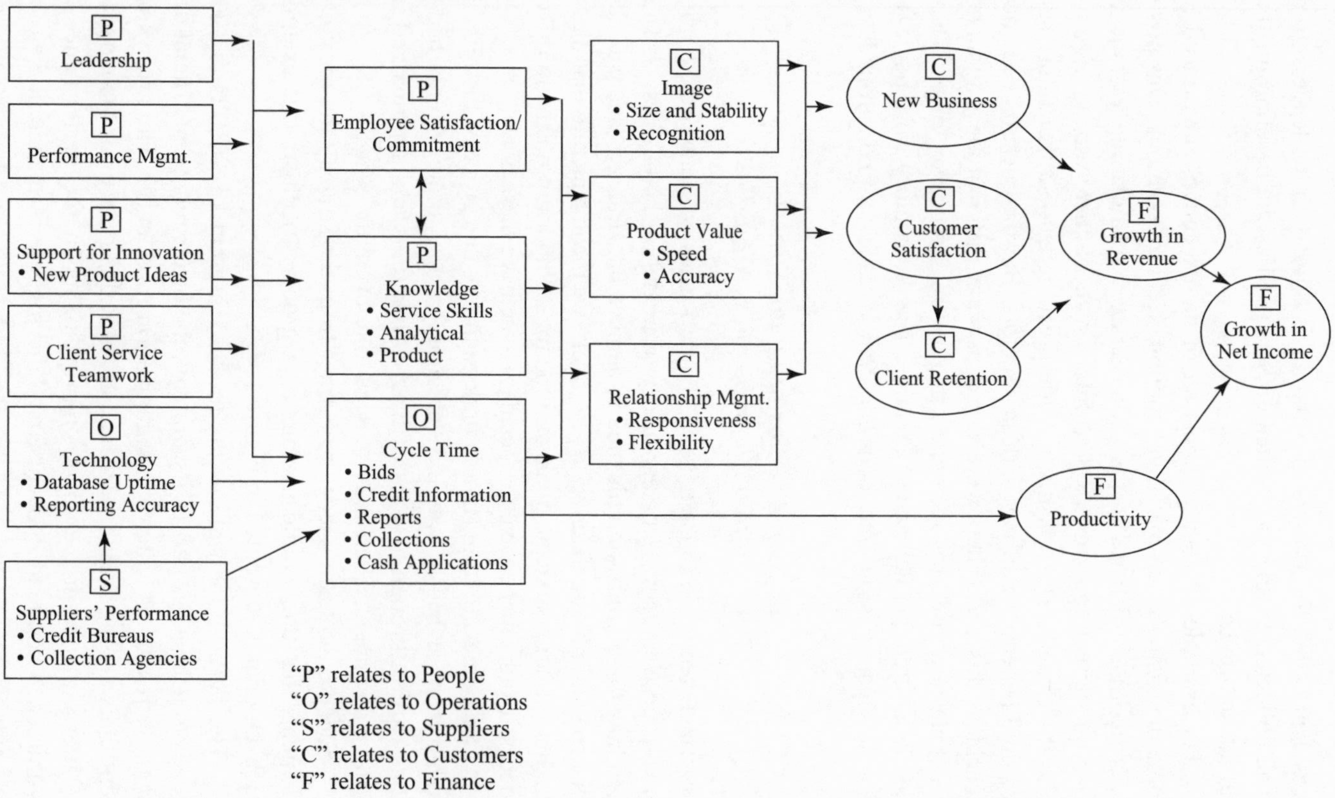

"P" relates to People
"O" relates to Operations
"S" relates to Suppliers
"C" relates to Customers
"F" relates to Finance

improve "customer satisfaction," the company would need to improve its "product value" and "relationship management."

Tuning in to the debate within Factex's leadership team can illustrate the types of issues that building the model helped to clarify. But before we do, keep in mind that the survey and interviews found that everyone on the leadership team agreed that customer satisfaction was key to strategic success and that improved relationship management with customers was an important driver of customer satisfaction. Both these points had been extensively discussed in the original strategy formulation debates. Unfortunately, a half-year's effort at Factex to improve relationship management with customers had produced mixed results.

The model-building effort at Factex gave the executives an opportunity to share perspectives on why greater improvements had not been made, and in so doing better align their thinking about the strategy.

Executive 1: *We all agree that improving customer satisfaction is absolutely key to our future success, and that in order to do that we have to improve customer perceived value of our products. Let's move on.*

Executive 2: *Not so fast. I'm not sure we have really agreed to a "strategic" approach to doing that. We talked about improving our products and customer service, but those seem like Mom and apple pie. Who can knock it? In my mind, the key strategic element for doing that is speed. We have to respond more quickly. It's been mentioned, but we haven't talked about it much as a group. I think it should be one of our very top priorities.*

Executive 3: *I agree. There are at least three major ways speed can help us Obviously, one is reducing cost. A second is making us look more responsive to the customer. But, there is a third. Speed of response influences which customers we are able to capture—and good customers are easier to satisfy than poor ones. The faster we move, the more likely we are to attract high-quality customers—the ones our competitors are trying to sign up. When we are slow, we end up with the poor credit risks—the customers others have turned down. I think cycle time has to be a key component of our model.*

Executive 4: *Fine. But, now that you raise the issue of the quality of our customers, there is another issue I think we need to clarify: what kind of image in the marketplace do we want? The best customers are looking for high quality, stable companies. They want partners that will be there in bad economic times, as well as good. Each year we invest a lot of money in various public relations efforts. I think we need to be more explicit in defining—and measuring—what we want those efforts to produce. What is the image we are striving to establish, and what is the main thing we want that image to do for us? We can't continue to spend the kind of money we do on PR and not include it in the model. Either it is important and we measure it, or let's spend less money on it.*

A senior team that holds such discussions and builds an agreed-to model that captures its best thinking about the business takes an important first step in deciding what needs to be measured. The process of building the model helps the senior team identify, and resolve, areas of disagreement. It also summarizes in one central place what they believe to be the most crucial elements of their success. In this regard, the model provides an excellent vehicle for communicating the strategy to employees. Finally, the model serves as a solid framework for deciding what needs to be measured to track successful implementation of the business strategy.

In the course of building the model, Factex's senior team also created behavioral definitions for each concept in their model. For example, one identified success driver in the people area was "knowledge and skills." What exactly did the executives mean by this? What were the skills? Who needed them? How would someone know if these skills were being developed and applied? Development of detailed behavioral definitions for each component of the model served several important ends.

First, it helped the leadership team members further identify areas of disagreement among themselves. By drilling down to the behavioral level, team members were able to identify areas in which their agreement at a broad level was not supported by a discussion of the details.

Second, elaborating the model's concepts helped the leadership team ask—and answer—the question: What are the positive and negative consequences of behaviors emphasized in the model and how can we achieve a balance in emphasis? For example, if a sales force is encouraged to track only sales revenue, this measure may well become the sole focus of attention, with the inevitable temptation of discounting prices and destroying margins. The revenue goal must be counterbalanced by a margin goal to avoid dysfunctional price discounting. Providing behavioral definitions to the concepts helped the leadership team identify areas in which there needed to be counterbalancing measures.

The third important reason for elaborating specific behaviors behind the model's concepts is to allow the leadership team to delegate and involve other employees in the measurement design process. The more clearly the leadership team is able to specify the behaviors for each concept, the easier it is for others to understand the team's strategic intentions.

Having spent significant time developing behavioral definitions for each concept, the leadership team at Factex moved on to a further consideration of how well the model achieved balance. The team explored balance from four different perspectives:

- Drivers versus results
- Short- versus long-term objectives
- "Soft" versus "hard" areas of performance
- Representation of the different interests among key stakeholders (investors, customers, employees, and suppliers)

The result of the leadership team's efforts during their off-site sessions was an initial model of the business with behaviorally defined concepts that balanced the needs of multiple stakeholders and provided both results and leading upstream indicators of strategic success. The model provided a rock-solid foundation for communicating the strategy and for deciding on a set of strategic measures that would allow the organization to monitor the progress being made in implementing its strategy.

The final task was to agree on the next steps. This involved agreeing to appoint several cross-functional teams to help decide the best way to measure the concepts in the model that had been so carefully defined. More specifically, the teams were established with two goals in mind:

- To design a reliable and valid set of measures to track how well the strategy model was being executed
- To build buy-in and commitment into the strategic measurement system throughout the organization

The leadership team completed the off-site meetings by agreeing to meet within forty-five days to review the work of the measurement design teams.

How Well did Factex Navigate the Key Gates

Phase I of the process was now completed at Factex. Before considering the experiences of some less successful companies, we should consider how the activities and experience of Factex compare to our key gates in Phase I.

The process employed at Factex contained a number of key characteristics that enabled the leadership team to build the foundation for a successful cultural change effort.

First, the initial scorecarding effort was undertaken by the leadership team, rather than being delegated too quickly to a lower level. This afforded several important benefits:

- It communicated a clear message to the rest of the organization that the scorecard effort was important.
- It helped ensure that the senior team would accept ownership of the measures and use them. At Factex, the leadership team came to own the measures through the sweat equity it invested in building the model.
- It developed supporters, and even several champions, for the process at the highest level of the organization.
- It provided a clear framework so that the leadership team could effectively delegate the measurement design to other employees in the next phase of the process.
- It provided the senior team with an opportunity to experience directly some benefits of the change process. To a person, the senior executives felt that their time had been well spent, that important issues in the strategy had been clarified, and that the model provided a powerful tool to help communicate the strategy. The benefits the executives experienced reinforced the likelihood that they would continue to support the process and develop attitudes that are consistent with a measurement-managed culture.

Second, members of the leadership team took the time necessary to de-velop a detailed strategic model before beginning to develop specific mea-sures. By reaching clear agreement on "what to measure" before debating "how to measure" it, the Factex executives avoided a source of common con-fusion. When executives begin talking about measures without a clear theory of the business, debates can quickly become unproductive. For example, prior to developing a clear theory of the business, two executives at Factex became involved in a debate that seemed to revolve around the technical issue of how to measure customer satisfaction. One executive believed *product attributes* such as price or functionality should be the focus of the measurement, while the other felt *service characteristics* should be measured, such as responsive-ness, ease of access to account executives, and professionalism of the service representative. While this exchange sounded like a technical debate, what was really being discussed was the strategic issue of competitive advantage. Did it revolve around cost leadership and product quality or unique levels of ser-vice? The what/how confusion can lead to endless debate.

At Factex the executives did a good job of avoiding the "what vs. how" trap by resolving the "what" question first, which is what Phase I is all about.

Third, the scorecard effort was led from the top of the organization. There is no doubt that the probability of success of any major change effort is directly proportional to the commitment and involvement of the top leader-ship. This fact is so important that at Factex it was not left to chance. The au-thors took time to provide personal coaching to several executives on their role and behavior in the off-site meetings. For example, during the prepara-tory interviews we learned that Factex's president felt so strongly about cer-tain issues that he invariably took control of the meeting whenever those issues were discussed. This shut down debate. We diplomatically advised him to make a special effort to listen first to the discussion on these issues before commenting. Commitment requires discussion, debate, and discipline.

SOME LESS SUCCESSFUL EFFORTS

The Factex case summarizes a successful process that we have seen played out in many organizations. Let's briefly look at some less successful ex-amples as an instructive contrast.

"Drag-It-Out, Inc."

The leadership team of this Midwest equipment manufacturer decided it simply could not afford several days off-site to work on strategy refinement and measures. Instead, the top team members decided to spend two hours at each of the next six monthly staff meetings reviewing and refining their strategic performance measures. Six months later, there was still no agreement on what to measure and, not surprisingly, time set aside for measurement discussion had slowly been usurped by other issues.

The two-hours-a-month process provided benefits at too slow a pace to sustain itself. In addition, the process that emerged was actually painful for the executives. We were told that each measurement discussion was cut short just as the executives began to warm to the task and tackle the real issues. Endless recapping provided less and less time for discussion. Faced with inconclusive sessions, growing frustration over making progress, and no clear benefits, the leadership team lost interest.

Drag-It-Out, Inc. paid the price of violating a central tenet of success: Keep the process moving and provide rapid benefits to sustain new behaviors.

"Pass-It-Off, Inc."

A large division of a major publishing company took a different approach to strategic measurement. The leadership team in this company decided that the best approach would be to appoint a cross-functional team of subordinates to develop the scorecard. The team was duly appointed and put to work. More than a year later, the team contacted us and asked for assistance. Little or no progress had been made.

The measurement design team had floundered for lack of a clear strategic model upon which to build a scorecard. These managers had made a bold start and created a list of measures that they felt captured important performance areas for the company. However, each time they met with the leadership team to review their work, they were sent away to try again. In describing the process, one committee member lamented:

> They turned us into a bunch of rock collectors. We bring our senior executives a rock; they look at it and tell us, "Not *that* rock." Then they send us away to look for another rock. They never

gave us a clear message about what was wrong with the rock we brought them, or what kind of different rock they want. They just made it clear they did not like what we had brought them.

The conversations between the cross-functional team and the leadership team were confusing. They tended to include both technical discussions about how to measure things, together with strategic discussions about what ought to be measured. The process proved to be frustrating and dissatisfying for everyone, and did little either to unify the senior team or to clarify murky areas of the strategy.

QUESTIONS TO THINK ABOUT

Here are seven questions that test whether or not you have successfully navigated the gates of Phase I:

1. If asked individually, would each member of the leadership team articulate the same key objectives for the measurement process?
2. If the president of the organization suddenly disappeared, would the senior team still agree on the strategy and theory of the business?
3. If asked independently, would each member of the leadership team identify the same limited set of key results and key drivers underlying the theory of the business?
4. Are the concepts in the model of the business well balanced between results and drivers, between short- and long-term objectives, and across various stakeholder perspectives?
5. Have members of the leadership team defined the key concepts in the model of the business in behavioral terms?
6. Has a plan been developed for executing Phase II of the project?
7. Have members of the leadership team put their personal time and energy into the process?

CHAPTER 6

DESIGNING THE MEASURES

How many times have any of us been part of or overheard a conversation examining the really deep questions of existence? You know, the kind of conversation in which one friend asks another, "What do you really want from life?" And the response might be, "Happiness."

Such an answer occupies the top rung on the ladder of abstraction.

The friend then inquires further, "What do you mean by 'happiness'?" And the response this time might be, "I want to be successful." This answer is a little more concrete, as the respondent takes one step down the ladder.

Gradually the responses become more specific. "I want a successful professional career." "I want that professional career to be in medicine." And "I want to achieve an above-average income level." So it goes.

As we descend the ladder of abstraction, our goals become clear and more specific. We open up the possibility of planning, taking action, and measuring progress. Clarity and specificity of the "what" makes possible an assessment of the "how to." When both are in place, success becomes likely.

While Phase I of developing a measurement-managed culture addresses *what to measure,* Phase II is concerned with *how to measure it.* Both are critically important. The most successful organizations we work with, like Factex, recognize that the "how" component of Phase II encompasses two key objectives:

- Identifying technically correct measures
- Building commitment throughout the organization to what and how things will be measured

Once again, let's start by examining the "gates" that successful organizations are able to navigate. These are illustrated in Figure 6–1. As with Phase I, there are four gates associated with successful completion of Phase II.

Gate 1: "Theory of the Business" Tested

It has been said that the higher up in the organization an executive is, the less he or she knows what is really happening. Maybe so. But what surely is true is that middle managers and individual contributors closest to the customer have an important perspective on what it takes to run the business successfully. Ignore this perspective at your peril. This is why the wisest executives seek to have the theory of the business that they developed in Phase I validated by other stakeholders.

Beyond improving the quality of thinking about the theory of the business, the testing process is essentially an opportunity for broader involvement. People become committed to things they have a hand in building. By bringing others into the testing process, the senior team assures greater commitment and ownership of the model and the measures that support it.

Involving others in testing the theory of the business also improves their understanding. Learning becomes active, rather than passive. Study after study has demonstrated the superiority of experiential, or activity-based, learning. Compare, for example, the difference in understanding between a group of managers who have read about building a business plan and those who have actually authored and defended one.

Gate 2: Valid, Reliable Measures Identified

There are many ways to measure the same thing. Some of them are good, others are less so. By "good," we mean that the measures conform to a set of key criteria. Table 6–1 identifies several key criteria for evaluating how "good" a measure is. In Phase II, alternative methods for measuring every aspect of the theory of the business need to be considered and the best measure selected according to the relevant criteria. Unfortunately, the choices are not always easy. Like many complex business decisions, several factors have to be weighed against one another in reaching the best decision. An example can help demonstrate how these criteria are applied, while at the same time illustrating the "art" involved in selecting a good measure.

Figure 6–1 The Four Phases for Developing a Measurement-Managed Culture

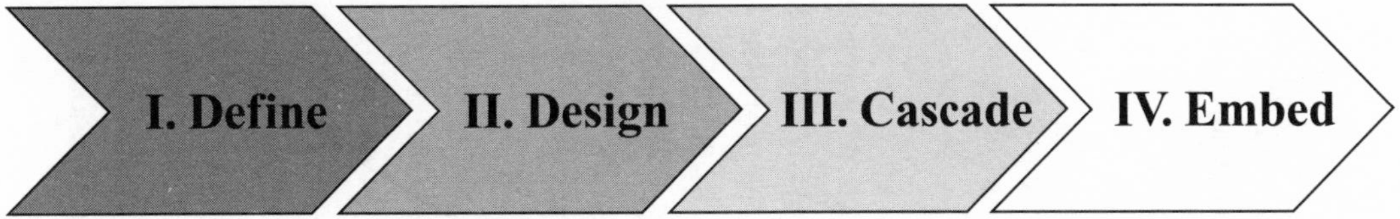

I. Define	II. Design	III. Cascade	IV. Embed
Gates:	*Gates:*	*Gates:*	*Gates:*
1. Clear process objectives formulated	1. "Theory of the business" tested	1. "Cascading" structure determined	1. Management process integrated
2. Agreement on strategy secured	2. Valid reliable measures identified	2. Strategy communicated	2. HR systems aligned
3. The "theory of the business" defined	3. Performance targets set	3. "Cascade" leaders trained	3. IT systems linked
4. Top leadership commitment secured	4. Process leaders developed	4. System of measures linked	4. "Theory of the business" refined
		5. Measurement behavior linked	

Table 6–1: KEY CRITERIA FOR GOOD MEASURES

Validity:	Does this measure really measure the intended concept?
Reliability:	Does the measure exhibit a minimum amount of noise or error, changing only when the underlying concept of interest changes?
Responsiveness to change:	Does the value of the measure change quickly when the underlying concept changes?
Ease of understanding:	Can the measure be easily explained and understood?
Economy of collection:	How much additional cost will be required to calculate this measure on a quarterly basis?
Balance:	Are the measures as a group balanced along important dimension? (For example: results vs. drivers, short vs. long term, across multiple stakeholder perspectives)

A diversified energy company that we worked with moved strategically to increase the number of products bought by each customer. Executives hoped that customers who bought electricity would also buy natural gas, propane, and oil from the company. In thinking about how to "measure" this concept, the design team first thought of calculating the average number of customers in a region who were using each of the company's products. For example, the measure might be calculated for the northeast region as displayed in Table 6–2.

One approach the team considered was having the high-level scorecard measure reflect the average score of the national sales regions.

By most of the criteria shown in Table 6–1, the measure seemed acceptable. First, it was reliable. There was not a lot of error or noise that would make the measure fluctuate if sales did not change. The measure also seemed sensitive to change. As more and more energy services were sold to clients, the numbers in each region would climb. The measure was also relatively easy to explain, and the information needed to calculate it was already being tracked, making regular updates economical. The measure seemed like a good one to many of the design team members, but it was not the measure they finally chose.

The company was organized around a matrix structure comprising both commodity managers, such as the vice president of propane sales, and geographical managers, such as the vice president of the northeast region. The geographical managers and their staffs maintained the primary account relationships with customers. The major opportunity to expand the number of products used by a customer involved having the geographical manager visit customers, perhaps accompanied by a product manager, to discuss needs in areas outside of the customers' current product usage.

The design team knew that it needed a measure with growth targets that would capture the "breadth" of products purchased by each customer, not simply the growth in number of customers. This suggested a slightly different measure: knowing how many products each individual customer was using. If these data were available, it would then be possible to compute for the region the average number of products being used by each customer. An example of this new approach is displayed in Table 6–3.

Table 6–2: INITIAL PROPOSED MEASURE OF CUSTOMER PRODUCT USAGE

Average number of customers in the northeast region using company products:

Natural gas	3,456
Oil	683
Electricity	1,432
Propane	333
Average for northeast region	1,476

Table 6–3: FINAL ACCEPTED MEASURE OF CUSTOMER PRODUCT USAGE

Average products used by customers in northeast region	
Customer	**Products used**
A	2
B	4
C	1
•	•
•	•
•	•
Last customer	3
Average products used	1.75*

*Sum of all products used in the region divided by number of customers in the region.

This measure appeared equally reliable, sensitive to change, and understandable as the first measure. It also had the advantage of measuring more directly the concept of "buying breadth"—the average number of products being used by each customer—than did the first measure. Design team members felt it would encourage the geographical managers to know exactly how many products each of his or her customers were using. This enabled the organization to grow the "breadth" of customer purchases—the strategic objective—rather than simply increase the number of customers, a more likely result of the first measure.

The one disadvantage was that the information needed to calculate this second measure was not currently being collected by the organization. Databases would need to be redesigned to calculate and begin tracking accurately the number of products being used by each of the organization's customers. However, this company felt the additional expense was worth the investment because it provided a better guide to the geographical managers. Both measures were good, but one was strategically superior as a communication vehicle to motivate employees toward desirable behaviors.

Gate 3: Performance Targets Set

The power of clear goals has been extensively documented. For example, James Collins and Jerry Porras in *Built to Last*[1] identify "audacious goals" as one of the key attributes that separate visionary companies from their less successful counterparts. The authors recount example after example of the role clear goals have played in driving organizational success. We do not wish to revisit where many others have traveled. However, a quick review of how specific goals contribute to the power of strategic measures is instructive. Goals can:

- Unify efforts of a work force and foster teamwork. Psychological research has demonstrated repeatedly the unifying power of goals for fostering teamwork.
- Further clarify strategic intent. Where can improvement be gradual? Where must it be breakthrough in nature?
- Force outside-the-box thinking, especially when breakthrough goals are established.

- Help communicate progress. How close have we come to our destination?
- Transcend leaders. Visionary goals should not die with those who first proposed them.
- Provide a magnet that actually increases motivation as one approaches it. Animals other than horses run faster as they near the barn.

Clear targets drive the effectiveness of strategic measures.

Gate 4: Process Leaders Developed

Phase I is directed toward aligning the senior team and building its common understanding and commitment to the strategy. Phase II involves extending this circle of alignment to other leaders in the organization. This next level of supporters will be needed to lead and propagate the measurement system throughout the organization.

One of the most consistent findings in our studies of employee attitudes is that employees find their direct supervisors more credible than senior executives. In addition, they most want to learn about things through direct communication with their supervisors. This extends to messages about the strategy and ways of measuring success.

The best way to gain the commitment of this next level of managers is to involve them in building the measurement system. As we illustrated with multiple examples in Chapter 5, changing behavior is the best route to changing attitudes. This is why it is imperative to get the next level of managers involved.

SUCCESS AT FACTEX

Navigating the gates of Phase II at Factex was achieved through five steps or sets of activities:

1. Measurement design teams are selected and trained
2. Design teams draft an initial set of strategic measures
3. Leadership team reviews and approves the draft measures
4. Necessary information is collected to establish strategic performance targets

5. Leadership team approves the measures and establishes performance targets

Step 1: Measurement Design Teams
Are Selected and Developed

The leadership team at Factex struggled somewhat in deciding how Phase II might best be executed. The company was experiencing a strong push toward cost cutting. In general, staff levels were lean. Many senior executives felt the organization would face a serious challenge if substantial numbers of leaders were pulled away from their jobs to work on the measurement system. A group of executives argued forcefully to limit membership in the measurement design teams to three or four technical staff members—controller, market researcher, HR director, and IT professional.

The president had a different vision. He argued passionately that more people needed to be involved—specifically people from the line operations. He maintained that the line managers who would use the measurement system needed to be intimately involved in developing it. The president foresaw that he would need a "sales force" to help him sell the measurement system to the organization. He intended to draw that sales force from leaders throughout the organization.

When faced with arguments that the organizational leaders did not have time to work on the measurement system, the president countered that he believed developing the measurement system was their primary job. He argued that he could think of no better way for leaders to spend their time than in clarifying the business strategy, identifying ways to track how well the strategy was being implemented, and communicating that strategy and tracking system to the organization.

At one point in the debate, the president commented, only half-jokingly, "What's the worst thing that can happen if we cloister a group of leaders to work on this task? Someone else in their organization will finally make a decision!"

After a spirited debate, four "design teams" were established. Each team would focus on developing a separate group of measures in each of the four areas represented in the top team's "theory of the business"—which included financial, market, operations, and people. Each team was to be led by an executive from the senior leadership committee and had as members six to eight leaders drawn from across the organization, including employees who were individual contributors. The teams were selected so that each of the major Factex business units would be represented, along with the major geographical locations. In this way, the president would have a "sales force" distributed across the organization to draw on when it came time to communicate the measures.

Each design team was given two assignments, first to review and validate the theory of the business, suggesting any needed changes, and then to develop recommendations—and cost estimates—on ways to measure the concepts in each team's area, such as client retention, employee satisfaction/commitment, and cycle time.

The teams were given thorough briefings before being sent off to complete the tasks. To propel them to a fast start, each received a half-day orientation on the strategic measurement process; the business strategy; the theory of the business created by the senior team; and key criteria for deciding the best way to measure results (see Table 6–1). In addition, each team included among its members a senior executive from the leadership team and an external facilitator with measurement design and strategy experience. Backed by this support, the teams were given four weeks to validate the theory of the business and prepare a set of recommendations about how the concepts outlined in the theory might best be measured and tracked.

Step 2: Design Teams Draft an Initial Set of Strategic Measures

Following orientation, the design teams began by examining the theory of the business. This process led to some refinement in the theory map. For example, members of one design team identified "bid cycle time"—the speed of providing a bid at a client's request—as a key success driver that appeared to have been omitted from the theory in the leadership team's initial effort. Design team members from the sales organization had recently become aware of several competitors who seemed able to respond more quickly to customers' credit requests by using new computer and communication technologies.

Led by the sales people, design team members argued and successfully convinced members of the leadership team that "bid cycle time" needed to be added to the model as a key driver of both new business and customer satisfaction, and of the organization's ability to manage risk. Slow response made Factex less attractive to creditworthy customers who could quickly find credit elsewhere, leaving Factex with less creditworthy applicants. Thus, the design teams played an instrumental role in expanding the business theory. In so doing, they significantly increased their ownership—an important step towards becoming effective advocates for the measurement system.

Several concrete steps were taken to ensure that the design teams effectively completed Step 2:

- Several of the senior executives attended the initial meetings of the design teams to discuss the strategy and the model of the business. Their presence helped communicate the strategy and theory, as well as the importance of the measurement initiative. As one design team member commented, "This is the first time I've seen four members from the exec committee in the same room at the same time. They must be serious about this stuff."

- Each team included as a standing member one of the executives from the leadership team. In this way, each team had a continuous bridge to the leadership group to help answer questions and summarize background discussions about the concepts behind the theory of the business. The senior executive helped to get the team back on track whenever members became uncertain about an element of the strategy. This participation by senior executives had a major side benefit. These executives gained a greater understanding about all the nuances relating to the top team's theory of the business, about which assumptions made sense and which didn't, and about the root causes of many business issues. If someone had asked them to join a group of employees in a different context, most would have replied with "too busy," "higher priorities," and "I know most of this already." This venue provided an excellent way to deepen senior leaders' understanding.

- Each team received training on how to design effective measures. This included how to use good measurement criteria to evaluate potential measures, as well as how to analyze the unit's unique measurement strengths and weaknesses. After selecting the strategic measure it wanted to track, one design team undertook a full review of all the measures that its unit was tracking. Team members found that there were measures in place that were tied to a strategy that had been formulated ten years ago. Other measures conflicted with the unit's mission and strategy. For example, the organization still gathered and tracked measures of job security and other "entitlement" areas on their employee survey. These concepts were antithetical to the culture of risk, high performance, and accountability that the organization was attempting to build. Like many organizations, this unit had several methods for adding new measures, but had never had a procedure for eliminating old ones. The evaluation criteria provided a means for doing this, and the design team took advantage of its new tool.

- The external facilitator on each team had extensive measurement experience in the subject area to help team members through the process. Our experience indicates that many managers are not comfortable with, or knowledgeable about, measurement, and that those who profess knowledge are often off base. Without expert facilitation at this step, many teams will reinvent the wheel, design overly complex measures, or recommend unreliable measures that are influenced by many things apart from changes in the underlying business concepts. Teams could also draw on the cross-industry experience of their facilitators, so they could assess best practice and innovative measures being used by other firms.

• Finally, the teams were provided with a template for reporting their measurement recommendations to the senior team and a clear target date for when these recommendations were due. The teams were not left to flounder. They were briefed thoroughly on their roles, provided strong communication links to the leadership team and facilitator, and given a tight timetable.

Step 3. Leadership Team Reviews and Approves the Draft Measures

Once the design teams had time to develop a draft set of measures—a process that took four or five days of work over a four-week period—a full-day meeting was held at which the four design teams presented their recommendations to the senior leadership team. Each measure was reviewed against the theory of the business and evaluated against other possible measurement approaches. A number of the senior executives argued against committing a full day for the discussion. One suggested that the measures should be circulated for comment and then returned to the design teams for revision. This executive failed to recognize the value to be gained from face-to-face discussions of the recommendations.

Let us illustrate this value by listening to one of the issues being debated. The discussion concerned how best to measure "client retention," initially identified by the senior team as a key driver of revenue growth. The design team recommended to the leadership group that an appropriate measure for this concept would be the "percent of clients who renew their contracts each year." The ensuing debate followed:

Executive 1: *Measuring contract renewal rates sounds reasonable to me. Can we track that? What about clients who have a couple of contracts with us? Are we counting clients who renew or the number of renewed contracts?*

Executive 2: *Wait a minute. I'm not sure I agree with that measure. The issue isn't just renewing existing contracts. If we are going to drive higher revenues, we need a higher percentage of each client's business. What we should be measuring is how many clients purchase additional services from us beyond their initial contract.*

Executive 3: *No, our real revenue growth will come from expanding into new industry groups. We just want to hold our base while we expand into new growth areas. Counting contract renewals is fine.*

Executive 1: *Are you saying we don't care about getting current clients to buy new products?*

Executive 3: *I'm not saying we don't care. I am saying that the real strategic thrust is to hold our base while we grow by penetrating new organizations. I don't want to put a measure out in front of employees that will cause us to spend time and resources trying to sell a lot of new products to existing clients. We have to focus the majority of our sales resources on selling to new clients. The wrong measure will get our people focused on our existing client base, rather than focused on finding clients in new industries. . . .*

The executive team had thought they were in agreement concerning the importance of "retaining clients." However, the debate about how to measure this concept illuminated the differences that existed on the issue of expanding business to the current customer base versus focusing on identifying new customers. It was a crucial issue for the business, since the ultimate choice would drive resource allocation and sales-force focus.

The senior executives had held several conversations previously about the importance of retaining customers and developing new customers in different industry sectors. However, it was not until they had to discuss how to measure the concept that they had come face to face with their disagreement. Chances are, the senior executives would have missed this important debate if they had not gotten together to review the measures.

In the end, members of the Factex leadership team found great value in the process of discussing the measures. The resulting debate was not something that could have been achieved by delegating it to a cross-functional team.

Step 4. Necessary Information Is Collected to Establish Strategic Performance Targets

Because of the clear direction and support provided to the design teams, the measures they designed effectively represented well the underlying concepts. Consequently, the Factex senior team approved most of their recommended measures. This was important because it rewarded effort and encouraged members of the design teams to continue investing time and energy in the process. Factex avoided the unproductive dance that often occurs when cross-functional teams end up making multiple "trips to the hill," only to be sent back with a poorly defined "rock" to redo their work. Such dances tend to lead to discouraged and cynical teams.

Either for cost reasons or as a result of clarifying its own thinking, the leadership team did request that the design teams make several modifications to their recommendations. However, at the end of the meeting, 85 percent of the scorecard measures recommended by the teams were approved by the leadership team. The remaining 15 percent were returned to the appropriate design team to address.

One of the returned measures was supplier partnering. The senior team decided it could not justify the cost of measuring all suppliers each quarter, and asked the design team to rethink a sampling approach. Another measure that required rework was innovation. The measure recommended focused on the generation of new ideas, but missed a strategically important gap for the organization—the ability to convert ideas into new products that were commercially successful. The measurement design team went back to the drawing board and later returned with measures and targets of product commercialization that were eventually adapted.

Once there is agreement on the strategic performance measures, members of the design team set to work to establish performance targets. Good target setting involves two important pieces of information: the organization's current performance or baseline on the measures, and best-practices information. Effective target setting requires knowing where you are and where you want to go. The most effective companies do not simply improve by "5 percent" each year. Rather, they gather information on where the competition stands and identify areas in which major improvement is needed to remain competitive. They test the realism of the measures against the hard rocks of reality by asking: "Have the measures ever been achieved? If so, under what conditions and with what capabilities and support? If we achieve these targets, will our strategic position be realized?"

The work done by the design team appointed to develop "people" measures at Factex illustrates the target-setting process. The leadership team had identified, and the design team had confirmed, "employee commitment" as a crucial driver of strategic success. The design team recommended that commitment be measured as part of an ongoing employee survey effort. The challenge was to determine where the organization stood today on employee commitment and how this compared to best-practice organizations.

Initially, several members of the design team suggested possible wording for survey questions related to employees' feelings of loyalty to the organization. The consultant facilitating the group stepped in to provide a short, proven index of several questions, together with normative data on how employees at different companies typically respond to the questions. In fact, several of the questions in the index matched questions from the Factex survey. In addition, one of the team members attended a seminar in which he heard a presentation on Federal Express's survey program. Talking to a FedEx executive after the meeting, the design team member learned how FedEx employees typically responded to the same questions covered by the Factex survey.

To determine where the organization stood on commitment, each design team member asked fifteen employees to answer the questions on the index. While not a perfect sample, the compiled data was enough for a rough estimate of where Factex stood on employee commitment.

Armed with this information, the design teams were able to make recommendations on possible performance targets related to commitment. As a one-year goal, the team recommended an average response on the commitment index of 65 percent favorable. After learning about the FedEx performance, the team members set a more ambitious three-year target of 80 percent favorable, even though it represented a seven to eight percentage point improvement each year. Without the FedEx comparison, it is likely that the team would have settled for a less ambitious target. Comparison is often the most effective way to raise the bar.

Table 6–4 provides principles for setting performance targets that are realistic, yet drive higher levels of accomplishment. For example, the first principle is in sync with research that shows that people are more motivated

Table 6–4: PRINCIPLES FOR SETTING EFFECTIVE PERFORMANCE TARGETS

1. Targets should require extra effort but not be debilitating.
2. Three-year targets can be most aggressive—more time is available for breakthroughs.
3. Limit the number of stretch targets. Each year focus on breakthroughs in one or two key areas, depending on:
   - *Value*—how critical is this area to achieving the business strategy?
   - *Gap*—what is the size of the potential improvement gap?
   - *Timeliness*—is there a natural order in which issues need to be addressed?
   - *Appetite*—is there energy and enthusiasm in the unit to attack this area?
   - *Skills*—are the skills available in the organization or can they be acquired?
   - *Best practice information*—what are the possibilities in this area?
4. Build a clear business case to communicate the importance of achieving stretch targets.
5. In looking at best practices information, go outside your industry.

when there is a moderate probability of success. For many people this creates a healthy or productive level of anxiety that enables them to be challenged and feel a sense of accomplishment. Goals too difficult debilitate rather than motivate, and those that are too easy lead to complacency.

Regarding target-setting principle two, Jack Welch of GE has been a master at creating challenges in a three-to-five-year horizon. He demands far more than incremental growth will provide. This requires people to think "outside the box" to examine new alternatives for achieving breakthrough targets.

Principle three recognizes that focus is crucial and that no one unit or organization can tackle too many stretch goals. Be selective, which is why principle four highlights the importance of providing a defensible rationale for why a particular breakthrough will be crucial to the organization's success.

Finally, change and stretch are most stimulated by comparison. It wasn't until employees at Xerox truly examined Canon's product reliability, operating processes, cost structure, and service delivery that they knew they had to change, and change fast. Employees on American automobile assembly lines did not see a quality difference between U.S. and Japanese models until they actually "broke down" Japanese cars and examined tolerances, fit, and reliability. We have seen few stimulants to change that are as powerful as seeing what the competition or potential competition is doing.

One other example serves to illustrate the power of best-practices information in thinking about performance targets. A client in the energy sector had been examining invoice costs, which stood at $16 per invoice. Checking other companies in the same industry indicated that invoice costs ranged from $15 to $19. Based on this information, the company seemed in pretty good shape, and not necessarily a candidate for aggressive improvement. However, the entire nature of the debate changed when someone discovered invoicing costs were less than $1 per invoice at Wal-Mart. Best practice information can create a greater awareness of possibilities and have a profound effect on goal setting.

Before meeting with the senior team to discuss targets, the Factex design teams undertook one final task that would greatly benefit subsequent efforts to introduce strategic measures to the organization. Members of each team reviewed their measures and recommended targets with other key stakeholders both within and outside the organization. For example, customer design team members met with several clients to discuss their plans for tracking customer value, client relationships, and corporate image. Did the measures make sense? Did the clients think emphasis was being placed on appropriate service attributes?

Similarly, the people and operational teams met to get input from several line managers who had not been involved in the measurement development process. Corporate board members were consulted on key financial measures to determine their comfort with the targets, as well as to seek their approval of the general theory of the business. It was important that the board buy into the key drivers of the business, since it would be involved in resource allocation and performance reward discussions.

In short, the design teams continued to build understanding and buy-in to the theory of the business, and to the measures that would be used to track implementation of the strategy.

Step 5. The Leadership Team Approves the Measures and Establishes Performance Targets

As the last step in Phase II, the design team members were reunited with the leadership team for final approval of the measures and to establish performance targets. Given the cross pressures on the leadership team, what was truly impressive was the lack of complaints from senior team members about the amount of time that they had invested in the effort.

Measurement cuts through the fuzz and forces specificity. Most members of the leadership team saw, firsthand, the power of measurement to clarify the strategy and to resolve important issues that had rarely been raised when strategic discussions had been allowed to remain at high-altitude, nosebleed levels. The fact that the president was actually immersed in the scorecarding process helped quiet the few chronic complainers on the leadership team and convinced them that discretion was the better part of dissension. After all, who could be busier than the president?

Measurement is more than a fuzz buster. It can also help to set priorities. Organizations can get themselves into trouble by trying to implement too many "good ideas." In today's pressure-cooker environment, an organization only has time to do the imperatives. In many cases, a good idea should not be implemented unless it is among the critical few things that the organization must do to be successful.

The target-setting effort at Factex proved to be an important additional step in helping the company decide what was really important. Aggressive stretch targets could not be established for every measurement area. In sorting out where the greatest effort would be placed, the senior executives were forced to make trade-offs.

Tuning into some of the debate illustrates how the process unfolded at Factex. The discussion that took place at the meeting revolved around the targets for improving the performance management system versus improving key technical skills in the work force.

Executive 1: *I think we really need to go after this skill issue. My best estimate is that only 30 percent of the key people have the technical skills they need to be effective in our future organization. We need to set an aggressive target on the technical skills measure for the first year, and then ratchet it up for the succeeding two years.*

Executive 2: *I'm not sure that's possible. We've already set an aggressive target for improving the performance management system. Training managers who will be involved in that effort will require one hell of an investment, both in real dollars and the time of our HR people. If the HR folks are invested heavily in performance management training, where are the resources going to come from for skills training in these other areas we're talking about?*

Executive 3: *Jim's right. We have to be reasonable with these targets, or the whole effort will lose credibility. What's going to happen during the first year? Should we focus on redoing performance management or the technical skills?*

Executive 2: *I think we'd be better off attacking the performance measurement issue first. That will help clarify what we expect from employees. Once the expectations are clear, employees will figure out ways to pick up the skills. If we don't set the expectations, what's to say they'll be motivated to use the skills? If I only get one thing, I pick performance management first . . .*

As illustrated by this debate over training, the target-setting debates, combined with the theory of the business map, helped Factex executives think through the order in which different performance areas needed to be addressed. For the first time the leadership team began to pay serious attention to the question of which initiatives needed to be "removed from the plate." This long-overdue discussion finally took place as a result of taking a more holistic view of the many areas in which improvement would be needed.

With the identification of a final set of measures and performance targets, the executives at Factex completed Phase II. Their efforts took less than two months.

How Well did Factex Navigate the Key Gates?

First, the early work of the design teams, the review meeting held to discuss the draft measures, and the discussions of the measures with other stakeholders helped validate the theory of the business. With a number of minor revisions, the model developed by the leadership team withstood the test of wider examination and debate. At the same time, in certain key areas the model was expanded and improved.

Second, with training and facilitation support, the design teams were able to identify an initial set of reliable and valid measures to track performance in key areas of the business. As we continue to track Factex's progress, we will see that a few of the measures needed to be modified. But though it wasn't perfect, the first set of measures provided Factex with a strong starting position from which to continue to build its measurement system.

Third, the design and leadership teams identified performance targets for each measure. These were based on best estimates of current performance and best practices. They were not simple "5 percent improvement goals," but rather tough choices regarding which performance areas needed to be attacked first and where aggressive targets needed to be set in order to compete effectively.

Finally, Factex was able to build additional commitment to the measurement effort. Several early doubters became supporters of the process as the strategy became increasingly clear and long-standing disagreements were resolved. As the leaders continued to commit time to the measurement process and gain value from their efforts, attitudes began to change regarding the value of the process.

SOME LESS SUCCESSFUL EFFORTS

What can we learn from some alternative, less successful approaches to Phase II?

"Broken Communication, Inc."

Top executives at one company we know did a fairly good job of outlining a theory of the business before passing off the task of designing measures to a lower-level cross-functional team. At this point, the process fell apart, primarily due to poor communication between the leadership group and the cross-functional team. The top executives failed to brief the cross-functional team effectively. None of the top executives took a permanent position on the design teams. Finally, the top executives were only willing to spend short amounts of time reviewing design team recommendations. Rather than taking time to debate recommendations, top executives relegated the review process to one agenda item at several monthly leadership meetings.

The consequences of this weak communication process between the leadership and design teams readily become apparent. First, the design team failed to do a good job formulating its recommendations. Poor communication with the leadership team resulted in poor understanding of the strategic intent which, in turn, led to a weak set of measures.

The weak set of measures meant that more, not less time was needed for the situation to be rectified. Unfortunately, the leadership team did not appear ready to devote the time and attention that the effort required. When the recommendations for measures failed to satisfy the leadership team, additional two-hour discussion sessions were scheduled as part of the leadership team meetings.

Unfortunately, since the meetings were held monthly, the delay tended to drag out the process for several months. Rather than becoming engaged in a crisp process that provided immediate value, the organizational leaders as well as the design team members became mired in a painfully long process that appeared to add little value. As their recommendations were rejected one after another, members of the design team lost interest in the effort. Some even stopped attending meetings. Six months into Phase II, *Broken Communication, Inc.* did not have a final set of measures or targets. Worse, rather than strengthening their commitment to the process, an increasing number of top executives were questioning the value of the effort. *Broken Communication, Inc.* faced a broken measurement development process.

"Same Old, Ltd."

It is often tempting to keep existing measures in place—or tweak them—rather than create new ones. This is especially true where the existing measures are somewhat aligned with the theory of the business. However, one design team we knew focused heavily on cost cutting, and as a result became obsessed with using existing measures. The result was a series of measures that did not fit the concepts contained in the underlying strategy.

The organization in question was a chemical testing group which sought to become more responsive to customer needs as a result of a strategic reevaluation. A common customer request was for faster turnaround. The design team was charged with recommending a measure of "customer response speed." It turned out that the organization's testing laboratories were already measuring the time between when a compound was first registered for testing in their facility and the moment the test was completed. Because this information was already available, the team decided to use it as a measure of customer response speed. Unfortunately, although inexpensive to track, the measure was not really a valid measure of response speed from the customer perspective.

Responsiveness from the customer point of view was the time between when the customer first picked up the phone to request a test to the point at which the test results were delivered back to the customer. This not only involved the time the compound was at the testing site, but the sample-pickup time and the time to prepare a report of the test results. These latter elements were not being captured by the existing measure. Very often, the time involved in these two activities took longer than the actual testing. The "easy," preexisting measure did not do a good job of capturing the strategic concept.

The lesson learned is important: Look to an existing measure, but only if it truly matches the strategic concept you are trying to measure. Do not try to force-fit a measure simply to save a few dollars, or your creative energy.

"Back Burner Enterprises"

As executives at Back Burner Enterprises began to staff its measurement design teams, executives resisted putting their best people on what seemed an activity that was peripheral to reaching next quarter's numbers. In the end, the design teams included too many employees chosen because an executive felt they were expendable, rather than because they were movers and shakers of the organization.

Mediocrity has consequences. The less-than-optimal composition of the design teams had several undesirable effects. First, the measures proposed by the team were not of the highest quality. This prolonged the process. The leadership team felt uncomfortable with many of the measures and sent the teams back repeatedly to the drawing board. This slowed momentum and raised questions. Rather than becoming increasingly strong supporters of the process, several executives began to wonder aloud whether or not it was possible to develop valid measures for some of the nonfinancial concepts.

As the process sputtered and was viewed as being staffed by employees of lesser talent, other employees began to shun involvement. Few considered the effort to be a major initiative. No one wanted to be involved in what appeared to be a looming failure.

Eventually, Back Burner Enterprises managed to develop a scorecard. However, it has not yet become a driving force of the organization. Not surprisingly, the senior executives have continued to encounter problems "selling" the process to the rest of the company. Unfortunately, there are few leaders at lower levels of the organization to help them in the sales efforts. Having been discredited, it is uncertain whether the measurement effort will ever reach its potential.

QUESTIONS TO THINK ABOUT

Here are five questions to test whether or not you have successfully navigated the gates of Phase II:

1. Has the theory of the business been discussed and validated by a representative sample of employees outside of the executive suite?
2. Is there a measure associated with each of the key concepts of the business theory that is:
   - Valid
   - Reliable
   - Responsive to change
   - Easy to understand
3. Does the final set of measures find a way to balance:
   - Short- versus long-term results
   - Leading indicators of success versus lagging outcome measures
   - The perspective of multiple stakeholders in the organization
4. Have clear performance targets been established for each measure based on current performance and external benchmarks?
5. Are the "movers and shakers" of the organization involved in the process and committed to seeing it completed successfully?

CHAPTER 7

CASCADING THE MEASURES

Let's assume your company has a strategy. Do you know *where* it is? Granted, this may sound like a silly question, but we are often amazed by the answer.

One of the authors worked with a company president who was concerned that his organization was out of control. He felt his executives and function heads seemed to be veering off in different directions. We asked if a strategy had been developed, and if so, how was it being used. "Oh, yes," replied the president, "the senior team spent three weeks working with an outside consultant developing the strategy. It's right here in my drawer." The president then proceeded to pull out a one-hundred-page document from his desk drawer. "Who else has the document?" we asked. "Only the five executives on our top team," came the response.

The president admitted that the *War and Peace*–sized strategy had to be "boiled down" to be useful, but "we just haven't gotten around to doing it."

We probed a little further. "Who else is familiar with the strategy? How is it being used in managing the business?"

The president admitted that, in fact, not much time had been spent reviewing or discussing the strategy since it had been developed six months earlier. Apart from occasional references at senior executive meetings, the strategy played little or no role in the day-to-day management of the business. This company's strategy, it turned out, was little more than a dust collector locked away in the desk drawers of the president and his top team.

One reason for the strategic secrecy was the president's fear that his company's strategy could be compromised by the competitive intelligence efforts of his organization's rivals. While such a potential threat always exists, strategic illiteracy within the organization is a much more subversive danger. If no one knows what the strategy is, how can it be effectively implemented?

The most effective employees we have encountered are those who understand the strategy and how their job connects to it. This understanding provides a framework for making decisions, allocating resources, focusing everyone's time and attention on the same targets, and building commitment.

Cascading strategic measures involves communicating the strategy and having units across the organization develop measures to track how well the strategy is being implemented. The most effective cascading efforts are those in which divisions and departments throughout an organization create measures that reflect how well they are executing their mission. Cascading removes the strategy from the drawer, brings it out into the open, and turns it into a living, vibrant instrument with power to align and focus the organization.

Like the other phases in developing a measurement-managed culture, the cascading phase involves several gates a company must navigate to be successful. These are summarized in Figure 7–1 and in the section that follows.

Gate 1: "Cascading" Structure Determined

The objective of Phase III, cascading, is to communicate the measurement system across an organization, so that functions or business units have strategies that support the high-level business strategy. More specifically, cascading should ensure that:

- The measures that the enterprise, functions, business units, and departments are using are aligned with one other—and the strategic measures for the enterprise
- Individuals and teams have measurable goals that are supportive of their unit's strategy

Figure 7–1 The Four Phases for Developing a Measurement-Managed Culture

I. Define	II. Design	III. Cascade	IV. Embed
Gates:	*Gates:*	*Gates:*	*Gates:*
1. Clear process objectives formulated	1. "Theory of the business" tested	1. "Cascading" structure determined	1. Management process integrated
2. Agreement on strategy secured	2. Valid reliable measures identified	2. Strategy communicated	2. HR systems aligned
3. The "theory of the business" defined	3. Performance targets set	3. "Cascade" leaders trained	3. IT systems linked
4. Top leadership commitment secured	4. Process leaders developed	4. System of measures linked	4. "Theory of the business" refined
		5. Measurement behavior linked	

The senior team needs to agree on which cascading structure makes the most sense for the organization. For some organizations it is best to cascade measures by function. In such cases, each function defines its role in the overall strategy and then develops measures that will track how well the function achieves its objectives, given its role in executing the higher-level strategy.

For other organizations an alternative approach may make more sense. For example, a high-tech firm we worked with had identified four key processes that define its long-term strategic success. A cross-functional team directed each process. In this case, because most employees were tied to these four processes, and these processes were representative of the critical competitive competencies, it made more sense to cascade the company's strategic measures to the core processes, rather than through functions.

Before cascading measures, the senior team must agree on the best structure for cascading the strategy and strategic measures. It is common management wisdom that structure should follow strategy. A structure that is right for one strategy may be wrong for another. The strategic scorecard is often a good tool for evaluating the appropriateness of the structure. The model or theory of the business—introduced in Chapter 5—which represents the business strategy, raises structural questions. What is the best way to organize and group resources to most effectively manage the model of the business? Many senior teams have a major "aha!" at this juncture.

One financial services firm had a long history of organizing and driving performance by functions such as credit, operations, account management, and sales. At this stage in the company's strategic scorecard development, the top team's first inclination was to cascade the measures functionally. The credit risk measures would be the responsibility of the credit department; service and customer value would fall to account management; transaction processing to operations; and revenue, expense, and profitability to finance.

As the executives tested this notion, it became readily apparent that their ability to achieve the scorecard targets would be better enhanced if they could organize themselves more effectively to manage the interrelationship of multiple drivers and results that currently resided within functional silos. For example, in the interest of reducing credit risk, credit managers would likely tighten credit policies to the point that sales reps and account development professionals would not be able to attract new customers or grow existing relationships.

The potential problem was solved by encouraging multiple functions to come together to create a value proposition for current or potential customers, and restructuring around geographic territories that integrated these interrelated functions. In fact, client value teams were created that included representatives from credit, operations, and account management to ensure that within each territory they were effectively managing the driver-result relationships in their strategic model.

The strategic model helped management to evaluate which structure would best implement the business strategy.

Gate 2: Strategy Communicated

Cascading involves having different groups within the organization develop their own goals, strategies, and measures to track progress on how well they are executing their strategies. Such groups can best accomplish this when they have a clear understanding of the enterprise-level or business-unit strategy. One early gate that needs to be navigated in the cascading process is communication of the high-level strategy, particularly those elements of it that relate to the roles required of other units in the organization.

Our experience working with the sales organization of a telecommunication company illustrates how a good understanding of the enterprise-level strategy can facilitate the cascading process. A key component of the company's strategy involved accelerating revenue growth by selling an established set of products to new customers. The geographically organized sales regions differed widely in terms of market penetration. Some of the regions were well established and the sales force had penetrated most sites within their geographical areas. There just weren't that many new customers.

Several of the region leaders, understandably, felt that the strategy of accelerated revenues from new customers was not relevant to their situation. This, however, was not the thinking of the senior team in developing the strategy. The senior executives felt that even within well-saturated sales regions "new" customers could be found, if not within current sites, then within other divisions of client organizations. Until this aspect of the strategy was understood, the regions could not effectively define their roles and develop related plans and measures.

The senior team realized that there needed to be a deeper understanding of the potential market and began holding dialogue sessions with region leaders to establish what the real potential was and how it could be exploited. After these sessions, region leaders were able to develop measures and plans that would address the strategy.

Gate 3: "Cascade" Leaders Trained

Once a company decides how the scorecard will be driven through the organization, the leaders of the units who will be involved in the measurement-development process must be identified. Typically, these "cascade teams" will consist of the head of a business unit or function and his or her direct reports.

The cascade teams will need to be oriented and trained. The amount of training will vary, depending on the extent of involvement of the team leaders in developing the higher-level measurement system. However, even when the team leader has been involved in earlier measurement development efforts, other team members will need to understand the strategic measurement process and what is expected of them. In addition, they will need a thorough orientation to the strategy and theory of the business developed by the leadership team. Finally, members of the cascade teams will require technical training on how to develop valid and reliable measures that effectively capture the business strategy of their unit.

Gate 4: System of Measures Linked

One of the most important determinants of how well a strategic measurement system operates is the degree to which measures that are cascaded throughout an organization link to one another. Every lower-level unit that has a scorecard should be able to recount how each of its measures is linked to the higher-level scorecard measures of its parent organization.

If the measures have been cascaded through multiple levels of an organization, the targets that each of the units sets should, in total, equal the target set at the highest level. For example, if a revenue number has been established for an entire organization and has been cascaded down to several business units, the sum of the targets set by the business units should add up to the revenue target set at the organizational level. While this seems clear-cut when dealing with revenue numbers, it is less so with other measures, such as those dealing with customer loyalty, safety, customers' perception of value, or employee commitment. Some negotiation may be necessary across levels of an organization to make sure that the targets set at the organizational level are truly supported by the targets established by the supporting levels within the organization.

One question we are often asked is: To what extent must strategic measures developed at support levels of an organization be identical to the high-level measures? Our answer is that the measures of supporting units should be similar and linked to the enterprise-level measures, but not necessarily identical. Supporting units in an organization need the opportunity to structure measures in a way that reinforces their particular objectives and mission within the organization. For example, the measures developed by a sales organization are not necessarily expected to be identical to the measures developed by an internal service function, such as human resources.

In many cases, however, the measures developed at the organizational level can be identical to those at the unit level. For example, if it is decided that superior leadership is important and a measure has been developed at the enterprise level to track the degree to which key leadership attributes are being learned and exhibited, it may well be appropriate for supporting units in the organization to use the same measure. In most cases, it would be inappropriate for a supporting unit to decide either that leadership measurement was irrelevant to its mission within the organization, or that it should measure leadership in a totally distinct way from how it was being measured at the organizational level. Thus many high-level measures can be brought down directly and included on the scorecards of lower-level units.

Organizations with effective measurement systems tend to have roughly 50 to 75 percent overlap of supporting units' measures with enterprise measures. These identical measures provide direct links to the overall strategic performance measures. But a unit must always be prepared to define how unique measures can be linked back to measures of the parent organization. For example, if a sales unit decides that one of its key measures is "number of new organizations contacted," and if that measure is not tracked at an enterprise level, then the sales unit must be ready to explain how the measure is linked to an enterprise-level strategic performance measure, such as revenue or market-perceived value.

Gate 5. Measurement Behavior Linked

The ultimate purpose of strategic measures is to change behaviors. This means linking organizational measures to individual and team accountabilities. For example, if departments are being asked to prepare action plans to address a particular problem, the plan should include discussion of how the actions are expected to affect the strategic measures. Similarly, if managers are reviewing individual performance goals, employees should understand how their personal accountabilities are related to department, unit, and organizational strategic performance measures.

The power of linking measures to activities is illustrated in a story told about Andrew Carnegie. It seems that while making the rounds at one of his steel mills, Carnegie turned to the day foreman and asked him how many tons had been produced that day. The foreman responded that six tons were produced. Carnegie took a piece of chalk and wrote a big "6" on the floor. Saying no more, he left the mill. Later that same day the night foreman arrived, and he asked the day foreman what the "6" signified. The day foreman said that he was not sure, but that Mr. Carnegie had written it on the floor after asking how many tons of steel had been produced during his shift. The day foreman returned the following day to find a line through the "6," and a "7" written next to it. Several days later, so the story continues, the night foreman arrived to find a line through the "7," and a "7½" in its place. They say that Carnegie returned several months later to find his original "6" had climbed to a "10"!

The story illustrates the point that monetary rewards are not always needed for measures to change behavior. What is needed is for people to understand how the numbers relate both to their job and the things they can influence. At the steel mill it was clear to all the workers that the number represented the tons of steel they had produced on their shift. This number was linked directly to their job behaviors. The workers' natural competitive spirit and desire to excel at what they were doing took over and resulted in improved production. Such a result would not have taken place if the workers had not been able to link the numbers to their own efforts. To be effective, strategic measures must be linked to individual and team efforts. Employees must be able to see how they can influence the numbers.

SUCCESS AT FACTEX

How was Factex able to cascade its measures successfully? The starting point, as we have suggested, was to agree on how the measures should be cascaded.

Initially, Factex decided that it would be best to cascade measures by function, a traditional approach for many organizations. Interestingly, after a year of working with their measures, leaders at Factex felt that they would be better able to maximize performance on the measures if they reorganized on a regional basis, with a few central functions supporting the regions. While Factex began by cascading its measures functionally, as a result of using the measurement system the company evolved to a system with both regional and functional strategic performance measures.

Once it had been decided *how* to cascade the scorecards, the next question was *who* would lead the effort? The most obvious candidates were the directors of each of the functions (and later regions), together with their immediate direct reports. These groups were designated as the "cascade teams."

Factex took the following steps to ensure that the cascade teams developed effective scorecards that were linked to the enterprise strategy, while also being linked to improvement initiatives and individual and team accountabilities.

Step 1: Orienting the Cascade Teams

Step one in the cascading process involved briefing the teams on the high-level strategic measures. To understand the measures, the teams first needed to understand the strategy. The Factex president himself led the briefings and asked for volunteers from among his top team to assist him at each site. He also invited members of the measurement design teams from each site to join him in the briefing. In this way, a broader band of employees beyond senior managers were available to lend their support to the process.

Significant thought was given to how best to present the strategy to employees. The intent was that the strategic measures would not only clarify the strategy, but would help link the strategy to department objectives and the personal objectives of every employee.

Factex decided to begin by having the president provide an overview of the strategy. This included the strategy map summarizing the "theory of the business" developed by the leadership team. Next, a series of charts were presented that were designed to help employees see the links between a general strategic theme, a measure, and specific behaviors that were expected to improve performance on the measure. An example is presented in Table 7–1. In addition, a trend graph was presented for each measure to provide a clear example of how the measure would be tracked over time.

For many cascade team members, the briefing session was the first time they had ever heard a senior executive discuss the strategy. There were many questions, not only about the measures, but why the leadership team believed a particular construct was crucial to the long-term success of the company. The briefings lasted an entire morning, followed by discussions over lunch.

When employees were asked at the end of the session what they valued most about the briefing, they mentioned, first, the opportunity to ask questions of senior leaders about the strategy and, second, the listing of specific actions and behaviors that were expected to improve performance on the measures. This meeting brought Factex's strategy to life.

One final important element of the briefing was the time that the president spent describing how the measures would be used to help manage the business. He described in detail his plans to hold quarterly meetings at which the measures would be reviewed and performance gaps would be discussed. This detailed description delivered an important message: Factex would use measurement as a central component in managing the business.

The orientation session at Factex was designed to motivate employees by addressing three of the drivers of employee behaviors: personal gain, peer pressure, and supervisory expectations. First, the sessions made it clear to employees that the executive team would keep asking them about performance against the measures and targets. Second, it was hoped that the presence of members of the design teams, all of whom represented the organizational thought leaders, would help motivate acceptance of the measurement process. Third, it was expected that over time everyone would learn the value of tracking both enterprise and unit-level measures to help improve organizational performance.

Table 7–1: LINKING STRATEGIC THEMES TO INDIVIDUAL ACTIONS

Strategic Theme	Measure	Individual Behavior Impact
Client Retention	Average number of months of continuous service of members of the current client base	• Respond quickly and completely to complaints or problems • Introduce new services to existing clients • Anticipate upcoming client needs and propose solutions
Strong Client Relations	Six-month survey requesting clients' ratings of our: • Knowledge of their business • Responsiveness • Effectiveness in addressing complaints • Frequency of contact	• Know the client's business • Provide something of value in each contact • Visit each client personally every 6 weeks • Have a single point of contact fully familiar with the client's account

Once the cascade teams understood the strategy, it was time to clarify their role in the process. Nothing was left to the imagination. Table 7–2 summarizes the charge given to each of the cascade teams. Activities and due dates for each activity were very specific.

After the team assignments were made and questions answered, a brief training session was held to provide instruction for team members in the following areas:

- Developing a high-level strategy map for their unit representing their "theory of the business" (See Figure 7–2)
- Deciding which enterprise strategic performance measures are relevant to their unit's mission
- Developing, where needed, strategic performance measures for the important success factors within the units
- Completing a summary template that documents each measure's definition, frequency of reporting, targets, and person responsible for tracking and reporting the measure.

Table 7–2: CHARGE TO THE DESIGN TEAMS

Activity
1. Understand the strategy and high-level measures
2. Identify and map the key drivers and results that will define your unit's success, given its organizational role
3. Identify which enterprise-level strategic measures can appropriately be incorporated into your scorecard
4. Develop new measures required for your local scorecard; be prepared to describe the conceptual links between any new measures you create and the enterprise strategy as described by the strategic performance measures
5. Determine current performance and "best practices" on your measures and set a performance target for each
6. Develop action plans for the three biggest performance gaps your unit faces on its measures

Each of the cascade teams was told to decide which of the Factex enterprise strategic performance measures would be appropriate for the team's scorecard. This depended on whether or not the measure was pertinent to its mission or role within the organization, and whether or not it was a measure that it could influence.

For example, the overall strategic performance measure of "leadership" was relevant to all functions. Effective leadership, after all, is important in any unit with employees. However, the high-level scorecard measure of revenue was not directly linked to departments such as legal and HR, since—unlike sales—they did not generate revenue. The HR department could be expected to drop the revenue measure from its scorecard and possibly substitute a more relevant measure. Recruiting effectiveness, for example, could be linked to the higher-level strategic performance measure of profit via "cost management." Recruiting effectiveness could also be directly related to Factex's strategic performance measures of "leadership" and "knowledge and skills."

Before each cascade team could proceed with the task at hand, team members had to agree on the mission, as well as the strategy for achieving that mission. As might be expected, the units differed in the degree to which they had reached such agreement. Some had well-defined strategies, others did not. In order to help the units reach a basic level of agreement on their mission and strategy, each was encouraged to develop a strategy map describing "the theory of their *function's* business." This was done by first sharing the high-level map that had been developed for the

Figure 7-2 Sample of Initial Cascaded Measures at Factex

Factex Scorecard

People	Operations	Customer	Financial
• Employee satisfaction	• Cycle time	• Client retention	• Growth in net income
• Leadership	• Technology	• Customer satisfaction	• Growth in revenue
• Teamwork		• Relationship management	• Risk profile

Account Executive Function

People	Operations	Customer	Financial
• Employee satisfaction	• Loan processing speed	• Client retention due to AE	• Account revenue growth
• Leadership		• Customer satisfaction with AE services	
• Teamwork		• Service quality	

Credit Function

People	Operations	Customer	Financial
• Employee satisfaction	• Credit approval speed	• Client retention due to credit	• Credit losses
• Leadership		• Customer satisfaction with credit policies	
• Teamwork		• Service quality	

137

entire organization, and then providing facilitators to help the units develop a map that would summarize their goals and drivers. The map each
team developed served, in turn, as the basis for its function's strategic performance measures.

Step 2: Facilitating the Teams

One of the advantages of bringing several cascade teams together for orientation was the presence of different kinds of support people, both internal and external. Several members of the leadership team were present to
provide interpretation of the overall business strategy; there were also outside experts with measurement expertise in the areas of finance, customers, and employees. As the cascade teams began their efforts, these
experts were available to answer questions and provide coaching on the
"state of the art" in each measurement area and on what other organizations had done.

The cascade teams varied significantly in the amount of support and
facilitation they required. Many wrestled with the task of deciding, first,
what the critical few objectives for their unit were, and then limiting themselves to the few drivers that would really make a difference to their success. The most difficult challenge in such situations is agreeing on the
"critical few." Any group can brainstorm a list of thirty actions needed to
achieve their objectives. Far fewer can whittle the list down to ten—or
fewer—drivers that will have the greatest impact on their success. The facilitators provided the most value by challenging the teams and insisting
that they agree on a limited set of items that, if managed well, would bring
success.

Many cascade teams took advantage of the involvement of senior executives by asking for their views on what role their function should play
vis-à-vis the business strategy. One conversation between the president
and the HR cascade team is typical:

HR Team Member: *We've been discussing HR's role in leadership development and the development of other skills the organization needs for future success.*

President: *Good! I definitely see HR playing a key role in that area.*

HR Team Member: *We're debating the key drivers and the relative role that recruiting and selection might play versus training. As you look to the future, how do you see the relative importance of selection and recruiting compared to training as ways to improve skills and capabilities, particularly as they relate to leadership?*

President: *That's a good question. We discussed it at the leadership meetings. Labor markets are very tight. I don't think that's going to change anytime soon. As you know, we have always promoted from within. We need to provide our own people with career opportunities, and we need people in leadership positions steeped in the values and operating mannerisms of this company. That says to me that training is going to be more important than selection in molding our future work force.*

HR Team Member: *We agree. At the same time, the position of training director has remained open for almost a year, and last year we actually cut the training budget. These don't seem like the actions of an organization that has training as a key strategic driver.*

President: *You're right. One of the things we haven't always done well is to allocate budget cuts strategically. We sometimes look for the thing that will least harm year-end profits, rather than the thing that will ensure our long-term success. Our hope is that by articulating, mapping, and measuring more carefully what is really critical to our long-term success, we'll do a better job in the future allocating scarce resources. Looking forward, I believe training will be a critical driver for developing leadership and other key skills.*

Given the information shared with them, access to top management's thinking, and help by skilled facilitators, most of the business units were able to make an effective start in developing a map representing a "theory" of their organization. This map served as a foundation for determining what each team would measure.

To make sure the teams had what they needed to be successful, each team was provided with a coach to answer questions and help resolve problems.

Step 3: Strategic Performance Measure Review and Integration

The final step in the Factex cascading process was a one-on-one meeting between the senior team and each of the cascade team leaders. The senior team reviewed the measures, targets, and action plans of each team before the meeting, and the president came prepared to discuss the review in detail. The president and other senior team members were not shy about asking questions that ran the gamut from the unit's strategy to how the proposed strategic performance measures related to the Factex strategy and strategic performance measures.

One of the president's central interests was the target set by each unit. Unit targets, when aggregated, needed to hit the overall company targets. In several instances, such as those dealing with revenue, the president challenged units to set more ambitious targets to help meet those of the organization. In other instances, the dynamic reversed itself: For example in the area of client retention, Factex targets were lowered to reflect business realities in the units.

The president and his senior team also called for revisions in several units' measures and action plans. For example, one operating unit created far too many measures. There was a fear that this could not be managed. Another unit adopted financial metrics that were not in line with the corporate formulas. The president was encouraging, but firm, concerning the depth of thinking and planning he expected. He left little doubt that he took this effort very seriously and expected the heads of each unit to do the same. A partial snapshot of the Factex cascading structure is depicted in Figure 7–2.

How Well Did Factex Navigate the Key Gates?

Stepping back to look at the cascading process, how well did Factex do in navigating the gates of Phase III? The strong involvement of the president and other leadership members undoubtedly helped Factex navigate the gates effectively.

The work completed earlier in Phases I and II, and the time the senior executives spent discussing how to cascade the measures helped ensure that the top team would communicate with the organization in one voice. The cascade teams heard a common story from the senior leadership members who attended the off-site meetings. The strategy map and other written materials reinforced their message.

The half-day spent both explaining the strategy and answering questions provided cascade team members with a solid understanding of the enterprise-level strategy upon which to build their own strategy and scorecard. The training and facilitation left no doubt about the importance placed on the effort by the president, or of his willingness to provide the necessary support for the teams.

The president himself led the effort to review and integrate the measurement systems of the units and ensure their linkage to key high-level performance targets. Finally, the insistence by the president that each team provide an analysis of ongoing initiatives and action plans to address three to four key performance challenges ensured linkage between unit scorecards, department actions, and individual and team accountabilities.

SOME LESS SUCCESSFUL EFFORTS

The Factex cascading effort becomes even more impressive when compared to a number of less successful efforts.

"Put-It-In Writing, Inc."

A service company decided it could not afford the time and money to bring its cascade teams together. Instead, the company decided to rely on the power of the pen to communicate the strategy and cascade team assignments. An information packet was prepared that, in fact, did a laudable job of summarizing the strategy, the scorecard measures developed to track the high-level strategy, and team assignments. The packets were distributed to division heads, along with a schedule for completing their unit measures. The measures designed by each division, however, were decidedly inferior to the Factex effort both in terms of content and commitment.

Several things went wrong. In general, there was a much shallower understanding of the high-level scorecard both by the senior leadership team and by members of the cascade teams. A written document cannot provide the richness of exchange that occurs in a four- or five-hour dialogue. At Put-It-In-Writing, Inc., many questions that existed in the minds of the division leaders went unarticulated and unanswered. The division leadership teams lost the advantage of hearing detailed explanations of the strategy. And, without the give-and-take of discussion and without the need to provide examples of the concepts behind the strategy, the top executives themselves never developed a deeper understanding of the strategy. It was not surprising that understanding and commitment to the strategy throughout this company was less successful than the Factex situation. This led to a weaker measurement system that was less well integrated with the strategy.

"Disengagement Dynamics"

Actions speak louder than words. One of the quickest ways to undermine any initiative is for the president, and other members of the senior team, to begin withdrawing from the process.

At an engineering company that is exactly what happened. Things began well. The president of the company and several other senior executives attended an initial kickoff meeting of the design teams. They remained at the meeting during a brief overview of the organization's strategy and answered a limited number of questions. Shortly thereafter, the executives headed for the door. In addition, the president delegated the assignment of reviewing the unit measures and action plans to a small group of organizational development specialists who worked in the HR department. The president spent little time discussing how the measurement system might be used to help manage the organization. Before long, the words "measurement system" simply fell off the chief executive's radar screen.

As went the president, so went the cascade teams. Although their efforts began well, as the project progressed, the teams spent less and less effort designing and refining their work. The message was clear: the president and senior leadership team had other priorities. With heavy schedules and intense pressure to perform, the interest of midlevel managers began to wane. No one was surprised when the measurement effort fizzled.

"Momentum Lost, Ltd."

In today's hard-pressed enterprise, loss of momentum is a deadly killer of new initiatives. In a relatively short period, the leadership team of an information technology company refined its strategy, developed a "theory of the business," and developed a high-level scorecard. At that point, budgeting season began, and all work on the scorecard ended. Almost three months went by before the organization felt it was in position to begin cascading the measures. Unfortunately, during the three-month hiatus the HR department had initiated a separate strategy communication effort. The first thing that the new communication consultant retained by HR did was to interview the senior executives about their strategic objectives and how to achieve them.

The communication interviews had the unintended effect of creating a whole separate system of results and drivers that were not fully aligned with the strategic measures that the leadership team had created three months earlier. Suddenly, the organization was confronted with two sets of objectives, one related to the strategic performance measurement effort, and a slightly different set related to the communication initiative. Unfortunately, top executives were inconsistent in their communications relating to the two efforts, and employees understandably became confused. Just as bad, the initial burst of energy for the strategy communications project overshadowed the measurement initiative. Despite an attempt at revival, the measurement effort continued to falter. It became another victim of lost momentum.

QUESTIONS TO THINK ABOUT

Here are questions you can ask to see how well your organization is navigating the gates of Phase III:

1. Do managers and others in the work force understand the high-level strategy and performance measures, along with the relationship between the two?
2. Are the top executives deeply involved in communicating the strategy?
3. Are senior leaders involved in reviewing both the supporting unit's scorecard measures and the rationale for how their managers will support the strategy?
4. Do functional and unit leaders have a clear understanding of the role their unit plays in supporting the parent-level organizational strategy?
5. Do middle managers have sufficient skills to design and implement a strategic measurement system for their units?
6. Is a process in place for linking strategic measures to local unit objectives and individual accountabilities?

7. When added together, do the targets set by supporting units assure that the enterprise targets will be met?
8. Is momentum being maintained? Who says so?
9. Will cascading of the measures to the next level be completed within a two-month period following the completion of measures at the next highest level?

CHAPTER 8

EMBEDDING THE NEW CULTURE

It is one thing to create a set of strategic measures and to "cascade" them so they are reflected in the way performance gets measured throughout the organization. It is quite another to make sure that the new strategic measurement approach takes hold. How do you sustain the change to a measurement-managed culture?

The challenge of sustainability is well demonstrated in the world of sports. Given advances in nutrition, training, and conditioning, professional athletes typically are in terrific shape. Yet, muscle, speed, and agility are not enough. Think about the legendary teams, such as football's Dallas Cowboys and San Francisco 49ers, baseball's New York Yankees, basketball's Chicago Bulls, and hockey's Montreal Canadiens. One reason these teams have won year after year is that their organizations possessed a unique set of values or culture—call it a winning philosophy—which sustained their competitive edge.

How do you sustain the initial sunburst of enthusiasm for strategic measurement so that it becomes a deep-seated winning philosophy and a driver of operational behavior and competitive success?

Embedding a culture is not quite so linear a process as some of the other changes we have talked about. As we have worked with different organizations we have witnessed much more variability in implementing Phase IV. While we will continue to follow the success at Factex as it moves through the embedding phase, we will draw heavily on other client experiences to illustrate points in the process.

The gates an organization must navigate in Phase IV are somewhat less well defined than they are for the other phases. But most of the successful organizations focus on the four areas summarized in Figure 8–1, as they move to embed a new measurement-managed culture:

1. Managing the business by the strategic performance measures—for example, setting priorities, reviewing initiatives, allocating resources, and budgeting by the strategic numbers
2. Linking human resource systems to the strategic performance measures—for example, performance management, rewards and recognition, training, and selection
3. Developing information technology systems to facilitate and support use of the strategic performance measures
4. Continuously improving the strategic performance measures—and the theory of the business

Gate 1. Management Process Integrated

Organizations that use measurement systems merely as a sidebar frustrate employees by asking them again and again to jump through hoops to gather and maintain information that is only marginally utilized. Measurement becomes powerful when it is integrated into the context of "the way we manage our business."

To integrate strategic performance measures into the day-to-day management of the business, keep the focus on four key goals:

- Make the measures a regular part of the management process.
- Use the measures to help set a limited number of clear priorities.
- Involve as many people as possible in a regular measurement review process.
- Review the measures regularly with the board of directors or the parent organization.

Let's look at each of these.

Figure 8–1 The Four Phases for Developing a Measurement-Managed Culture

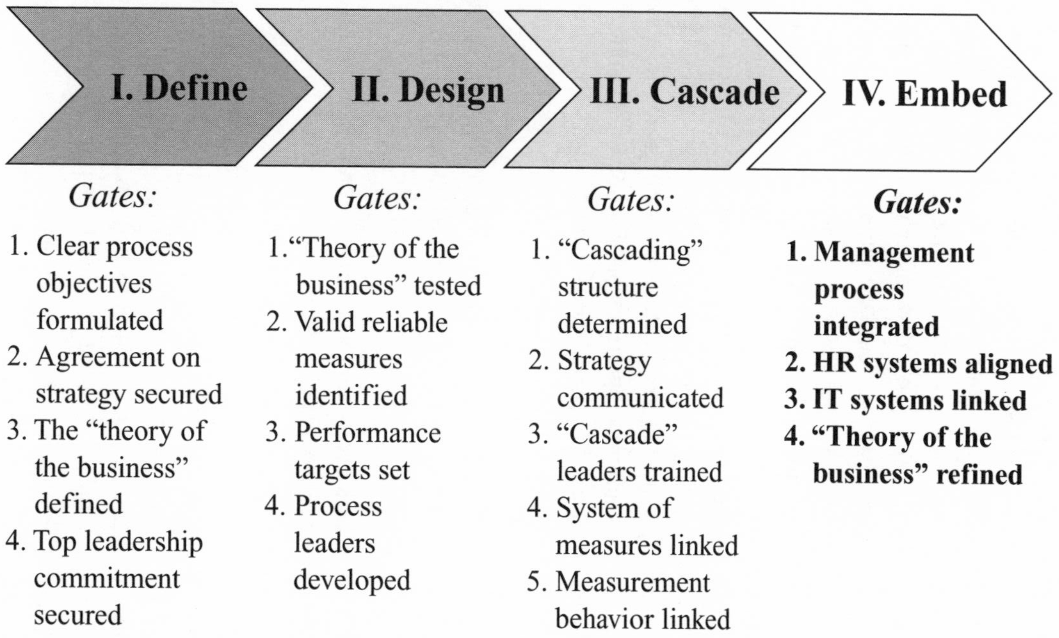

I. Define	II. Design	III. Cascade	IV. Embed
Gates:	*Gates:*	*Gates:*	*Gates:*
1. Clear process objectives formulated	1. "Theory of the business" tested	1. "Cascading" structure determined	1. Management process integrated
2. Agreement on strategy secured	2. Valid reliable measures identified	2. Strategy communicated	2. HR systems aligned
3. The "theory of the business" defined	3. Performance targets set	3. "Cascade" leaders trained	3. IT systems linked
4. Top leadership commitment secured	4. Process leaders developed	4. System of measures linked	4. "Theory of the business" refined
		5. Measurement behavior linked	

147

Make strategic performance measures a regular part of the management process. At Factex, the president instituted quarterly review meetings at which performance on both the organizational and divisional measures was reviewed. Since discussion time was limited, all measures were circulated before each review meeting. Meeting time was devoted to discussing the four or five most challenging strategic performance measures for each division. Following a review of the organizational measures, each division discussed its biggest challenge area. A division spokesperson described key gaps and their causes, what initiatives the division was taking, and what milestones were in place to evaluate whether or not the analysis was on point and the corrective actions were working.

This process significantly changed the nature of the Factex executive meetings. Previously, most discussions in the meetings had been tactical in nature. Debates had tended to focus on such issues as miscommunications and rivalries among departments, glitches in account management, and staffing changes. Problems were brought up only when they were solved, thereby translating them into epic tales of success. Unsolved problems had been kept underground.

As the strategic performance measures became pivotal, a more strategic set of questions captured increasing amounts of executive time. For example:

- Which elements of employee satisfaction are most closely linked to providing high levels of customer satisfaction?
- Where is structure blocking the organization's ability to maximize performance on the strategic performance measures?
- Do the market research data provide any indication that the company is beginning to improve its image as a market leader among midsized customers? What links can we see between this improved image and our ability to attract better customers?
- Are the improvements in customer satisfaction translating into higher customer retention?
- What tells us that employees understand the strategy better and are focused on improving the strategic performance measures?
- What kind of changed behavior are these measurement review meetings generating?

Factex's management process began to foster an environment in which challenges to a competing point of view were based on facts, there was greater experimentation with new solutions to problems, and hypothesis testing became a risk-free activity.

One of the most crucial requirements for managing any business with strategic performance measures is to make sure that the performance numbers are updated frequently. If you want your managers to achieve a particular result this quarter, measure it this quarter; if you are unconcerned about when the result should be achieved, measure it every two or three years. What gets measured frequently, gets managed frequently.

When the authors conducted employee surveys two decades ago it was generally accepted that employee surveys needed to be repeated only once every twenty-four to thirty-six months. The rationale: "That is how long it takes to change employee perceptions." Furthermore, changes of 5 to 10 percent in employee favorable ratings over a two-year period were viewed as a major accomplishment.

Things surely have changed! When Factex moved to more frequently measuring and reviewing results, it witnessed the following percentage increases in favorable ratings on their employee survey in only twelve months:

- Teamwork and cooperation (+27%)
- Fairness in administration of policies and procedures (+26%)
- Confidence in senior leadership (+19%)
- Effectiveness in implementing new ideas (+33%)
- Performance management (+42%)

Managing a business with strategic performance measures means more than making them a regular part of the management review process. It also means effectively managing capital flows and allocating resources by the numbers, which in turn require careful priority setting. This brings us to the second goal.

Set a limited number of clear priorities. Many organizations run into trouble by trying to accomplish too much too soon. Little gets accomplished and invariably performance fails to improve.

The authors once worked with a troubled Midwest manufacturing company whose president was asked to step down shortly after our arrival. While things were bleak, there was one division that was able to grow its profits year after year.

Over dinner one night we asked the head of the standout division how he had managed to be so successful while everyone else was falling apart. He replied that each year he met with his leadership team and asked its members to select just two objectives to achieve during the coming year. A good deal of time was spent debating which two objectives would be selected. Once the two objectives were chosen, the team riveted its attention on accomplishing them. The division president believed that this focus allowed his organization to build on its strengths and become very successful. Results proved his point.

Fifteen to twenty strategic measures can easily point to a host of performance gaps. A leadership team's first response may be to try to fix them all at once. Our recommendation is, don't. Rather, pick a manageable number of high-priority objectives for the year. One or two may be enough, if they are the right ones. By addressing top priorities continuously year after year, an organization will build on its strength and be well on its way to successfully implementing its strategy.

To help in its prioritization process, a global laboratory services organization we worked with began to ask each of its divisions to prepare a chart like the one in Table 8–1. Across the top of the chart each division was asked to list the measures on its strategic scorecard. Divisional executives were next asked to highlight the three or four measures that they felt would create the biggest challenge for them in terms of achieving their targets (the shaded measures in the table). Down the rows of the table each division was asked to list all the initiatives and programs it had underway that would require significant resource expenditures, in terms of both time and money. Where the rows met the columns, the divisions were asked to place an "x" if executives believed the initiative would have a major impact on helping to close the gap. Of special interest was the expected impact each initiative would have on the three or four "high-challenge" targets the division had identified. The initiatives with the greatest impact on these areas would receive the highest priority. The initiative grid is designed to help each unit focus on a limited set of objectives that are most important to its success and that of the company as a whole.

This ranking of initiatives had a second beneficial consequence: It suggested to each unit actions that might be put on the back burner. Companies have many ways of putting new initiatives onto managers' plates. For the first time, managers in this global services organization had a mechanism for *de-prioritizing* an initiative. Units were encouraged to eliminate—or postpone—initiatives they did not perceive as likely to have a major impact on helping them close a priority performance gap. For example, initiatives relating to outsourcing which affected only one priority gap area were given a low priority until additional resources became available and other higher priority initiatives were secured.

Involve as many people as possible in the regular review process. If strategic performance measures are to become the cornerstone of the day-to-day management of the business, employees at every level must begin to use them. To encourage this, Factex's president included almost fifty managers in his regular review process, compared to the dozen or so that were traditionally invited to senior management meetings. Data for each meeting was prepared well in advance and circulated so that the strategic performance measures review team was prepared to use meeting time to wrestle with issues, not simply to report information.

The review meetings have had several positive results. First, they have enabled the fifty most influential people in the business to understand on a continuous basis where the organization stands in implementing its strategy. Second, because input is solicited from a wider group of people, there has been earlier identification of issues that keep the organization from achieving its target performance. These reviews became dialogues about the findings, not pro forma dog-and-pony shows. Successes are celebrated and gaps are thoroughly discussed. Third, the meetings enabled the top fifty executives to communicate to their units similar messages about the strategy, current performance, and the initiatives being developed to address problems. By keeping critical issues top-of-mind for the very people who can effect change, Factex won an important battle in its effort to transform itself.

Table 8–1: INITIATIVES GRID

	Strategic Performance Measures*							
	Financial					Customer		
Initiatives	Customer Revenue	Net Retained	Customer Value Added	Revenue/ Employee	Capital Efficiency	Market Share	Increase in Major Projects	Market Perceived Value
PS upgrade					X		X	
Add'l experienced manpower to service group								
Acquisition of laboratories in new market sectors	X		X	X	X	X	X	X
Penetrate new organizations	X		X		X	X	X	X
Add'l supplier-partnerships	X		X			X		X
Outsourcing initiative			X					X

*Strategic Performance Measurements that are below target are shaded.

Review strategic performance measures regularly with the board of directors or parent organization. Finally, any organization that is managing the business with strategic performance measures should regularly share performance on the measures with the board of directors or parent organization, as is done at Factex. Better yet, the board should have its own set of strategic measures. Motorola, for example, has a set of measures for its board that reflects its role in guiding the business for the long haul. In our experience, management teams that treat strategic performance measures as a set of ongoing accountabilities to their board or their parent typically achieve higher performance when compared to firms whose reporting and review process are sporadic and only internal.

In fact, a major distinguishing feature of high-performance organizations is the accountabilities that are created for key strategic measures

Table 8–1 *(continued)*

Strategic Performance Measures							
Quality			Operations	Tech.	People		
Non-conformance Status	On-Time Delivery	Customer Shipments Off-Spec	Routine Testing Efficiency	New/ Improved Technology	Safety	Improved Skills	Satisfaction and Commitment
X	X	X	X	X		X	
X	X		X			X	X
				X			

from top to bottom. High performers tend to link accountabilities to everyone up and down the organization and tie them together with strategic measures.

Sears is a case in point. During the 1980s, Sears rhetorically committed to customer service but it did not link accountabilities to metrics that reflected its new philosophy. Nothing happened. In the 1990s, after Arthur Martinez arrived, Sears sought to become a "compelling place to work, shop, and invest." This time, Sears put teeth into its slogan with measures and accountabilities that it began to review with its board of directors. Performance took off.

What happens when an organization does not incorporate its strategic measures into the day-to-day management of the business? Contrast Regional Bank, which also developed a strategic scorecard, with the success at Factex and Sears. Regional Bank was an organization accustomed to moving quickly, so no one blinked when the executive team gave managers forty-five days to cascade its strategic measures and to develop annual plans based on their unit's measures. Plans were presented and approved. At the end of the year, the organization had met 60 percent of its scorecard targets including all but one of its financial targets. Not bad. Nevertheless, the senior team stopped using the scorecard the following year. Regional Bank's efforts to incorporate its new measures into management of the business went nowhere. What happened?

Senior executives began with the laudable goal of doing a better job at meeting customer requirements—a central requirement for maintaining the bank's competitive position. The first major piece of market research arrived in February suggesting that the company was information poor at customer-contact points. For example, when a customer used more than one service-contact point, bank personnel could not discover what other relationships the bank might have with the customer. Executives moved to correct the problem by pouring money into a customer information system. The investment turned sour because Regional Bank failed to evaluate how development of the system would be affected by initiatives in other strategic performance areas.

In April, data from the employee survey suggested big gaps in training, professional development, and diversity. Once again, the organization launched into new initiatives, slowing the prior customer information project. Additional data throughout the year continued to divert the organization so that its early commitment to improving customer information management took nearly two years longer than planned to complete. Such distractions and delays occur when strategic measures are not used to take an integrated view of how resources are being managed. Tactical issues begin to dictate strategic ones.

When measures are associated with this type of "stop-and-go" management, cynicism sets in and middle management begins to view the measures as just another *programme du jour*. Not surprisingly, Regional Bank's financial performance dropped and it became an industry also-ran. Managers became defensive. Finally, the bank's board of directors stepped in. The bank was eventually sold for two-thirds of the previous year's book value.

There are several key lessons in Regional Bank's experience. The most fundamental of these is that Regional Bank was never able to position the strategic performance measures as a central management system. Once put in place, strategic measures were rarely referenced. Business decisions did not employ the measures to evaluate the impact of important decisions on various aspects of the organization's performance. Resources were committed without referring to the full set of measures. At best, the measures were a thermometer collecting "nice-to-know" information. And like any passive recording instrument, the strategic scorecard did little to affect the business. It was business as usual with the added burden of collecting additional, marginally useful information.

The neglect of the measures led relatively quickly to disenchantment on the part of middle managers, who originally had hoped the system would be a means for focusing the organization and for providing desperately needed feedback to senior management. Once the scorecard effort was viewed as just another "program of the day," it was doomed.

Gate 2. HR Systems Aligned

One of the authors once consulted with the sales force of a Canadian computer manufacturing company. The sales organization had a powerful measurement system, tracking revenue, product margin, the number of contacted organizations, repeat sales, and customer satisfaction. Furthermore, the organization had recently doubled its sales training budget. Yet sales were consistently falling below target, particularly during November and December. What was going wrong?

Lengthy discussions with the sales people revealed that a major part of the problem was how the bonus system was administered. There were good bonuses for sales people who hit their yearly target, and the amount of the bonus increased significantly for a short time as a salesperson increasingly exceeded the target. However, the bonus curve flattened out quickly, not paying corresponding percentage increase as the sales target was exceeded by large amounts. Worse, sales targets for the upcoming year were set on the basis of a percentage increase over the current year's performance. Therefore, when a salesperson surpassed his or her target by a large amount, the result was a relatively small increase in bonus, but a big increase in next year's sales goal. Consequently, it was to a salesperson's advantage to surpass his or her yearly target, but not by much. Not surprisingly, many November and December contracts were being delayed until the new year. Once the bonus system was adjusted to better reward an outstanding sales year, the organization's numbers started to get back on track.

Few people want to perform poorly. Too many human resource systems operate by punishing 90 percent of the employees who are doing their job well in an attempt to control the 10 percent of borderline performers. Peak performance organizations find ways to unleash the potential of the 90 percent by better rewarding, recognizing, and supporting their efforts to achieve measurable success.

Here, we want to address three primary human resource systems that are the most crucial for supporting a new measurement-management management process: performance management; selection and development; and reward and recognition.

Performance management systems. Regional Bank and Factex present an interesting contrast in their approaches to aligning HR systems. While Regional Bank failed to focus on the link between its performance management and its strategic measures, Factex adressed the issue head on. Based on its strategic employee survey, Factex learned that from employees' perspective there existed numerous gaps and inconsistencies between the company's performance management system and the strategic performance measures.

Although a majority of Factex's employees understood their work assignments, few understood the business strategy or saw how their annual goals linked to it. Moreover, both coaching and feedback on performance happened sporadically. When it did occur, it appeared more tactical than strategic in nature. Although Factex had modified its performance appraisal process recently, the survey provided feedback suggesting the process was not delivering what was needed to drive the strategic performance measures.

Based on what it learned from its survey, Factex took specific action to rebuild its performance management system so that it would support and reinforce the use of its strategic performance measures. This was one of the best investments that Factex could have made. According to the vice president of human resources, a member of the leadership team, linking performance management to strategic measurement was an essential element of a successful strategic performance measurement process.

For Factex, the new strategic performance measures, coupled with a redesigned performance management system, created a powerful way to make progress in important areas that were previously not measured. Such areas as leadership, growth and development, core values, and internal customer value had previously been debated only in the abstract. Now, longer-term objectives within these areas were defined by concrete measures, cascaded throughout the organization, and discussed at individual performance reviews. While employees continued to keep their eyes on short-term financial and operating measures, they now had a mandate to improve performance in areas crucial to the company's long-term success.

Regional Bank unfortunately never linked its strategic measures to department and individual performance goals. Its performance management system continued to focus for the most part on activities, rather than outcomes, and included many nonmeasurable commitments for which results were almost nonexistent. For example, rather than focusing on important outcomes such as customer retention, and key drivers such as forty-eight-hour problem solving, the bank's account executives had performance goals that were too vague to be useful. A goal such as "complete service training to encourage customers to use a broader array of products" did not adequately focus attention on key business outcomes. Not surprisingly, the bank's strategic performance measures never really connected with those responsible for implementing the bank's strategy on a day-to-day basis.

Selection and development systems. Most companies do not do a good job of anticipating future skills, and are even worse at developing a focused set of new competencies. A strategic performance measurement system, if developed and implemented correctly, illuminates current and future competencies needed for success. These competencies provide a strong blueprint for selection, placement, and development systems. Once identified, these competencies must, in turn, be measured and managed.

Table 8-2: CORE COMPETENCIES REQUIRED TO SUPPORT ACCOUNT EXECUTIVE ACCOUNTABILITIES

Competencies for: Account Executive Position	Accountabilities for Account Executive Position					
	Negotiate Contract Renewals	Problems Resolved in 48 hours	Service Account	Credit Quality	Secure Premium Pricing	Introduce New Products
Customer/Client Focus	X	X	X			
Interpersonal/ Relationship Skills			X			
Planning and Self-Management			X			
Results Orientation		X			X	X
Self-Confidence and Decision Making	X	X	X	X		X
Analytical Skills	X			X		
Negotiation Skills	X				X	X

Shortly after developing its strategic performance measures, Factex set out to map the competencies it would need to achieve its performance objectives.

Table 8–2 outlines these competencies for the position of account executive, mapped against the position's accountabilities. One set of competencies, negotiating contract renewals, typically involves the account executive in negotiating new loan terms to reflect changed business conditions, changes in the client's credit worthiness, or possibly changes in the company's policies or pricing. The account executive must balance the goal of retaining profitable clients with securing favorable terms for the company. This requires good negotiating skills, a strong ability to analyze and communicate the client's financial position, and self-confidence to make decisions that are fair to both the company and the client.

By making explicit the competencies required to perform in a key position like account executive, which in turn supported the corporate strategic performance measures, Factex was able to create a broad map of competencies it needed to successfully implement its strategy. This allowed

the company to evaluate competencies that were weak across the organization and to commit resources for enhancing training programs where they
would do the most good.

The approach taken at Factex to identify and develop key competencies stands in contrast to what happened at Regional Bank. The bank did
have in place a set of defined competencies, including a list of "required"
managerial skills. However, the list was not linked to the bank's new
strategic measures. Nor was development of the competencies measured.
Managers were confused about how the list of competencies fit into the
strategic measurement picture. Since their development was neither being
measured nor rewarded, the statement of competencies was put in folders
and filed away.

Linking performance management and competencies to high-level
strategic performance measures is one of the toughest challenges organizations face. In the Appendix we have provided a more detailed look at
how Factex and some other organizations have made these connections.

Reward and recognition systems. In recounting the turnaround of
Continental Airlines in *From Worst to First,* Gordon Bethune comments
on a company philosophy that directed many of the airline's cultural
change efforts:

> Your employees are very smart. They pay close attention. What
> you're measuring and rewarding, they're going to do. So even if
> you define success right but you still measure and reward the
> wrong thing, your employees are going to figure out what you
> are measuring and give you that.[1]

If a strategic measurement system is to drive change in a sustained manner, it needs, ultimately, to be tied to the reward and recognition system.
There are several reasons why.

First, there is a strong tendency for people who are trying to change
behaviors to revert to older, habitual ways of doing things. As demonstrated in the classic Hawthorne studies that were conducted in the early
twentieth century, people respond to new interventions with new behaviors.[2] But without reinforcement, these new behaviors slip over time. So it
is with new measurement systems. Their introduction will tend to elicit

new behavior. However, if people feel that these new behaviors are not re-warded, they will slowly revert to old behavior patterns.

Second, in many cases existing reward systems may actually conflict with the new measurement system. This sends mixed messages to em-ployees. While the measures suggest one type of behavior, rewards rein-force alternative behaviors. The Canadian computer organization we mentioned earlier is an example of just such a situation. While the com-pany sought to maximize sales, there existed a disincentive to close deals in November and December, since it reduced the chances for a large bonus the following year.

Linking rewards, especially compensation, to a new measurement sys-tem is tricky business. If not handled carefully, it can undermine even those measurement systems with great potential. And with good reason.

New measurement systems can be threatening to executives and man-agers, many of whom have been successful as a result of their drive to control the environment. Typically, their success has resulted from an abil-ity to control the existing measurement system. Changing that system cre-ates new rules and great uncertainty. Until managers are comfortable with the consequences of the new system and their ability to influence them, they are likely to resist efforts to implement these systems. Linking pay to the numbers before executives and managers reach a minimum level of comfort amplifies their discomfort and may well lead them to reject the new system.

The experience of a retail company we know illustrates the dangers of moving too quickly to link pay with new and unfamiliar measures. A cor-nerstone of the company's strategy was to entice customers to buy more products in a product category each time they entered the store. A mea-surement system was initiated—and immediately linked to executive com-pensation—that tracked how many products each customer bought in the category.

It was a good strategy and a good tracking mechanism, but trouble was brewing. For a while performance on the measure improved, but then suddenly the improvement plateaued. Because the measure was linked to compensation, it attracted a good deal of attention when it stalled. Initial finger pointing was directed at the sales force, which was accused of not having sufficient fire in its belly. But the sales force fought back and suggested that the finger of blame be redirected to the folks in inventory control who just couldn't keep the right sizes in stock.

On the positive side, because the new measurement system was linked to compensation, it increased the speed with which the problem was recognized and addressed. Unfortunately, the measurement system died in the process. As a result of open criticism and attacks from other executives, both the vice president of sales and the vice president of operations who managed inventory became archenemies of the new measurement process. They were successful in derailing further deployment.

The purpose of introducing a strategic measurement system is to help managers evolve to greater heights, to think more strategically, and to succeed. If executives and managers are to accept and continue to use a new measurement system, it is important to have them avoid feeling overly threatened in the early stages. This may mean delaying for a period certain actions—like linking pay to measures which are likely to raise anxiety to an excessive level. Those who use the measures to attack other executives by outmeasuring them miss the point. Using measurement as a club causes fear and ultimately subverts the system.

How do we get managers to embrace new measures? First, by helping them to understand the importance of the measures to both their success and the success of the organization. Second, by helping them to understand how the measures work. Most managers will need to experiment with new measures to learn how the underlying concepts work and how they can best be managed. These are people who are used to succeeding. As a new set of rules are introduced they need time to learn how to succeed with them before the stakes are raised too ambitiously.

We typically recommend at least a one-year trial period before strategic performance measures are linked to executive compensation. A successful electronics firm with which we worked began by linking compensation to its financial and operating measures once the measures were well understood by managers toward the end of year one. In year two, compensation was linked to customer perception measures; and in the third year the company linked pay to performance on its people measures. This "go-slow" approach enabled managers to develop and become comfortable with the newer measures before they were "in the game" for their paychecks.

In thinking about when to link compensation to strategic performance measures, "time since the measures were introduced" is less important than being able to successfully navigate several developmental gates. These are:

- Having managers understand how the concepts being measured, and the measures themselves, relate to the business strategy—that is, why are the measures important?
- Educating managers on the basic nature of the measures. This includes such questions as: What is the historical baseline of performance? What are world-class benchmarks? How do we vary within our own organization on this measure? What are reasonable ranges of performance?
- Having managers understand what drives change in the measures and the concepts underlying them. Also, what is the managers' level of control in the change process?

Answers to these questions enable an organization to determine if managers are ready to accept linking a new measurement system to compensation. Acceptance requires people to believe that they can influence the numbers. They must also be confident of current performance levels and believe that the targets are attainable.

One final point is important relative to measures and compensation. Employees will become frustrated and begin to ignore metrics that they believe are unrealistic. Initially, employees will work very hard to attain established targets or rewards, but if they begin to believe the rewards are unattainable, they will become cynical, and stop focusing on them. To avoid this problem, we recommend setting one- and three-year performance targets. This enables managers to establish aggressive, but achievable, targets in the short term, while really stretching the team for the longer term. The longer three-year period provides the team with time to invent and test new approaches. In fact, some organizations with which we have worked have created pay differentials for the short- and long-term performance, paying a greater premium for achieving the longer-term, breakthrough performance targets.

The electronics manufacturer we mentioned earlier set up its executive compensation to reward for performance on their strategic measures on a rolling average over a three-year performance. This longer performance cycle reduced the focus on short-term objectives. This is especially beneficial in a rapidly growing organization where executives typically move to a new position every few years. Since the compensation level reflects success over a three-year period, an executive is less likely to mortgage the future of his or her department for short-term gains.

Gate 3: IT Systems Linked

The advent of the modern computer has driven home the distinction between data and information. Data are about facts; information—and knowledge—are about meaning. Computers are indiscriminant in their handling and displaying of data versus information. Organizational leaders need to be more discriminating. Most organizations are awash in more *data* than they can effectively use, while they often lack the *information* they need to manage effectively.

Winning with a knowledge organization and establishing a measurement-managed culture requires effective *information* management. *Data* management is a necessary, but not a sufficient, piece of this process.

What does effective information management involve? An increasing number of organizations are using new web- or network-based technologies to manage and communicate strategic information. What does this look like at some of the leading measurement-managed companies?

An organization we know in the energy sector has a system that will alert managers via their PCs whenever a strategic measure has been updated. Once the manager goes to the measurement area on the network, the first thing that appears is a complete relationship map displaying the "theory of the business." Key concepts in the map are labeled and colored-coded red, green, or yellow to reflect performance against targets. When the manager passes his or her mouse pointer over a concept in the strategy map, links among concepts in the map light up in different colors to show which connecting concepts drive—or are driven by—the concept under the pointer. This way, the manager can see at a glance how a change in performance on one concept is expected to drive—or be driven by—changes in performance on other concepts.

Table 8–3: ROSENBERGER'S LAWS OF INFORMATION

Law 1:	Faster information drives out slower information
Law 2:	Inexpensive information drives out expensive information
Law 3:	Information directly delivered to the customer drives out information not directly delivered
Law 4:	Content-rich information drives out content-lean information
Law 5:	Customized information drives out uncustomized information
Law 6:	Timely information drives out untimely information
Law 7:	User-friendly information drives out less user-friendly information
Law 8:	Secure, stable information drives out less secure, less stable information

Source: Joseph L. Rosenberger, "Answers are Easy," *Across the Board,* April 1997.

In addition, at the click of a mouse, a manager can access a written description of a concept, graphs comparing current performance against targets, historical trends, and measurement results from supporting units.

Joseph Rosenberger[3] has articulated what he proposes to be irrefutable laws of information transmission. These are displayed in Table 8–3. Incidentally, the system we have just described conforms quite well to these laws.

How well does your strategic information system conform to Rosenberger's laws? If you find that the communication of strategic information does not conform to Rosenberger's laws—for example, your key strategic measures are not being communicated quickly, relatively inexpensively, and delivered directly to managers—then there is a high probability that your managers are not using critical information effectively.

At a broad level, there are three major classes of information technology tools that companies are adopting to support their strategic measurement efforts:

1. *Systems modeling and statistical analysis* programs used to help build and test the model of the business. Such tools are being used both initially to test alternative scenarios of a business model and to test the correlations among different concepts in the model once measures begin to be collected.

2. *Information delivery and display* software to bring information to managers' desktops in a user-friendly fashion. This includes such things as graphical display programs and "push" or "web-casting"

technologies that make it possible to deliver messages directly to the desktop without them being requested.

3. *Data mining or warehousing software* that can help an organization gather and manage data.

While it is not within our purview to review software packages, it is worth discussing briefly some of the key criteria that need to be considered when designing an information system to support a measurement initiative. At a minimum, the system should possess the following capabilities:

1. Present and link information together in multiple formats, including flow charts, written text, tables, and graphs. The system should be able to communicate a story about the strategy or theory of the business, how success is being measured, and where the organization stands today relative to targeted performance.
2. Easily deliver output in multiple formats—colored computer displays are sexy, but there are times when a manager will need old-fashioned paper or overheads as output.
3. Enable users to move easily up and down the organization's information chain so performance gaps can be investigated at the appropriate level.
4. Expand easily and economically so that as the organization cascades its strategic measures to multiple functions and levels, the additional information load can be handled without reconstructing the system.
5. Provide levels of security so managers can view their own information before it is shared with the rest of the organization.
6. Track and compute correlations among different data points to help test and refine the "theory of the business."
7. Connect to the organization's already-existing information in a relatively easy fashion.
8. Provide easily accessible information—employees need to be able to retrieve information about strategic performance measures when they want it, not when someone in the IT organization has time to send it to them.

When we speak of "aligning information systems," we are not only talking about installing new computers and software. When Gordon Bethune began the turnaround at Continental Airlines, he invested heavily in computer systems to track and project capital flows more accurately. However, the channel he chose to distribute key strategic measures to employees, such as "on-time arrivals," was old-fashioned bulletin boards placed in every break room and updated on a daily basis.

The most important result in a measurement-managed culture is that information explaining the strategy and its implementation will be user-friendly and easily accessible to employees. Organizations that truly value strategic performance information frequently update information and make it readily available. Computers can automate some aspects of the process, but automation is not an end unto itself.

A final note on data mining or warehousing. Computers have long held the promise of allowing an organization to understand both strategic and operational challenges at a much deeper level. Retail stores, for example, can track to the paper clip what is happening with their inventory, including who bought what, during what time of day, with what credit card, following how many previous purchases, and on and on. Such information can be "warehoused" and subsequently sorted in an infinite number of ways to resolve business performance questions. For many organizations, however, data warehousing seems to have become a lost promise, if not a bottomless money pit. Trying to design a system capable of storing an infinite amount of data in an infinite number of ways can quickly become excessively expensive.

A strategic measurement system can help address the problem of a warehousing effort run amok. The strategy and theory of the business, in effect, provide a limiting framework that can help a company become more focused in its data warehousing efforts. Rather than trying to build a system that is all things to all business needs, the system can be designed to extract, first and foremost, information about the strategic imperatives. The increased focus that this provides can greatly reduce the cost of a data warehousing effort and provide a much quicker return on investment. More and more organizations are likely to find data warehousing a sound investment when it can be combined with a strategic measurement framework.

Gate 4: "Theory of the Business" Refined

We have been asked more than once, "How often should strategic measures change?" The correct answer is, only when your strategy changes. In fact, if an organization finds itself changing measures every few months, most likely its measures are more tactical than strategic.

A change in strategy should lead to a reexamination of the business model, and in turn to an adjustment to the measures or targets being used to track implementation of the strategy. At Factex, executives review the business model and strategic measures annually in conjunction with reexamining the business strategy. During this review process, Factex executives examine such questions as:

- Do the measures indicate that we are on track and that our strategy remains a viable one?
- If we fall short of our performance targets, what is the problem? Has the external environment changed and compromised our strategy? Did we overestimate the organization's competencies and capability to change? Is there a flaw in the business model we developed, or has our tactical execution of the strategy been poor?
- Have we been able to update the measures in an accurate, reliable, and cost-effective manner?

A negative answer to any of these questions will require adjustments to the strategic measures or their targets.

While theory says strategic performance measures should change only when the strategy and model of the business changes, real-life practice is slightly different. Most organizations that have developed a new set of strategic measures find that changes need to be made, particularly during the first year or two, as experience with the measures is acquired.

The experience of Sears is a good example of this process. Early in its measurement effort Sears was able to show empirically that retail locations with high employee satisfaction were able to generate greater customer satisfaction, which in turn increased customer retention and improved the bottom line. Sears began to ask employees a series of questions on a regular basis, which it combined into an "employee satisfaction index" to help retail outlets predict and manage customer satisfaction. Over time, Sears found a more limited subset of questions that most directly predicted customer satisfaction, enabling them to simplify their employee survey.

The initial business model created by an executive team represents a hypothesis about how the business will work. If the measurement development process has been an effective one, this model will have been refined and validated by the opinions of others in the organization. However, the model remains a hypothesis that needs to be tested against the harsh rocks of business reality. This testing occurs through successive updating of the measures and through statistical analyses designed to determine the strength of the correlations among the various measured concepts in the model. Over time, both the model and the measurements that support it need to be continuously tested and refined.

QUESTIONS TO THINK ABOUT

This chapter has highlighted the key factors that need to be considered to embed strategic performance measures into the cultural fabric of the business. Here are several questions that will help you determine how well your organization is navigating the Phase IV critical success gates:

1. Is there a clearly established management process for reviewing, analyzing, and acting on strategic information?
2. Do employees or teams have a set of accountabilities that are linked to their unit performance measures, which are then linked to the organizational strategic performance measures?
3. Is there a process for helping individuals understand how their personal performance objectives relate to the strategic performance measures?
4. Is there a process that links the development of key human resources and technical capabilities to the strategic performance measures and strategic performance gaps?
5. Do managers have access to strategic performance measures when they want it—not when the IT department decides to distribute them? Are the summaries accurate, friendly, and structured to communicate information, rather than data?

6. Are both the executive compensation system and employee incentives aligned to pay out when performance on strategic measures is high?
7. Is the model of the business and strategic performance measures reviewed on a regular basis, together with the viability of the business strategy?

CHAPTER 9

FROM MEASUREMENT MYTH TO MEASUREMENT MANAGED

G etting results, managing change, and measuring performance are all part art and part discipline. Mastering that art and discipline is essential for business success.

Some executives are doing it right. For them strategic measurement does not present a paradox but a way of managing and getting results in the new business environment. In Chapter 1 we briefly mentioned William Crouse who several years ago was president of a $500 million Johnson & Johnson subsidiary, then called Ortho Diagnostic Systems Inc. (ODSI), which provides a case in point.

To serve its customers and maintain market share, ODSI hit its markets with a dizzying array of products. Its sales force devoted as much attention to small customers as it did to those with greater potential. All of this pointed to a lack of strategic focus, which usually translates into higher operating costs and profit margin deterioration.

In addition, ODSI's organizational structure produced functional thinking and rivalry. The culture was risk-averse, turnover was high, and morale was low. Clearly, the company needed to change in order to maintain its leadership position in the competitive diagnostic segment of the global health care marketplace.

So change it did. The strategy became more focused, and there was a greater responsiveness to customers and less product and market clutter. Once the transformation began, turnover was arrested, volume more than doubled, profits skyrocketed, and morale improved.

According to Ortho's people survey, overall satisfaction with Ortho increased 24 percent over the two-year transformation period, communication improved 26 percent, innovation shot up by 45 percent, and employee assessment of management was up 41 percent.

How did Crouse and his ODSI colleagues achieve the turnaround? Through a systematic process which began with setting vision and strategy, and included diagnosing the organization's structure, systems, culture, and capabilities for strategic fit. Each of these elements was calibrated to align with the strategy and one another. The process hinged on a new strategic measurement system for tracking results and updating action plans.

This system provided managers with a handle on many of the people issues that were key to ODSI's turnaround. The measures provided feedback on teamwork across products and departments, competencies, leadership, communication, commitment to the strategy, systems effectiveness, customer focus, and change implementation. Armed with this information, Crouse and his team were able to increase focus, speed product development, and reduce cost and inefficiencies.

By this point, the benefits of strategic measurement should be apparent. They include:

- Better bottom-line financial results
- Greater customer loyalty, higher employee satisfaction
- Close alignment between the business strategy, marketplace opportunities, and the internal organization, including processes, structure, systems, capabilities, and culture
- Real commitment to organizational goals that comes from cascading strategic performance measures through the organization
- Accelerated organizational learning that is achieved through continual reviews and updates of the theory of the business
- Better balance of the often conflicting needs of different stakeholders such as employees, shareholders, customers, suppliers, and regulatory agencies

- Sharper focus on the priorities leading to better resource allocation, reduced initiative overload, and speed in decision making
- Having a common language which links the roles of every employee
- Integration of all diagnostic and tactical measures, and an end to measurement proliferation

But before you reap the benefits of measurement management, a little myth busting may be in order.

Over the years we have encountered several measurement myths that crippled the effective use of measurement. We present these below, with thoughts on how you can puncture these myths as you move toward the art and discipline of getting results, managing change, and measuring performance.

MYTH 1:
MEASURE "HARD" RESULTS AND THE "SOFT" STUFF WILL FOLLOW

You can learn a lot from an organization by paying attention to the goals it sets. In a national survey we conducted, two-thirds of the organizations reported setting financial and operational goals, but less than half of them set goals for the "soft" issues relating to managing people, suppliers, customers, and innovation. Despite all the windy rhetoric about "loving" customers, empowerment, and learning organizations, not many executives are willing to put measures where their mouths are.

There are exceptions. Johnson & Johnson, for example, realized years ago that financial results are essentially driven by how well executives manage key stakeholders such as customers, employees, and relations with the communities in which they operate. They carefully measure performance related to these stakeholders and educate managers and employees about the connection between delighted customers, satisfied and productive employees, good community relationships, and financial success.

It is dangerous for top management to focus on financial and operating results and measures and then "empower" lower-level managers to take care of the rest. If top management doesn't provide discipline for the "soft" areas, why should managers down the line?

Contrary to the first myth, financial results are outcomes largely dependent on "soft" employee attitudes and behaviors. As the measurement-managed companies in our survey have discovered, business success comes from paying attention to the hard and soft areas of performance, knowing how to link both, and cascading measures in both areas throughout the organization.

MYTH 2:
MEASUREMENT IS
FOR BEAN COUNTERS

Back in the salad days when top management could spend time at the corporate retreat opining on matters strategic and leave operational issues to the hoi polloi, measurement was left to the bean counters in finance and the production and quality control folks on the plant floor. Big mistake! While leaders at senior levels need not bury themselves in statistical process control charts, they can benefit by paying attention to the *strategic performance measures* discussed in Chapter 1: Markets, Financial, People, Operations, and Environment.

Senior executives need to set top-line measures of performance and lead the cascading effort to translate these measures into operational criteria throughout the organization.

MYTH 3:
MEASUREMENT IS
TOO REAR-VIEW ORIENTED

Remember Lot's wife, who turned into a pillar of salt because she looked back? It's a helluva price to pay for not looking ahead, and it may be one reason why many senior executives avoid the subject of measurement. Too often, measurement is used to record the past, not anticipate the future. This is especially true of most financial measures, and yet they continue to be used as the primary vehicle for meeting shareholder and regulatory demands.

One way to make measurement more forward looking is for top managers to review their strategic scorecard and ask: Do we have measures that can serve as early warning indicators of future problems? Or better yet, and less defensive in thinking, do we have measures that can signal future opportunity?

At one large supplier of medical services to hospitals, senior executives consolidated the company's two sales forces that serviced large and small hospitals, respectively. Initially, measures from surveys of the sales force indicated concern within the sales force of mounting customer dissatisfaction. Sometime later, the service system received complaints from customers about late product delivery and lack of responsiveness. Almost a year after that, we were asked to survey the hospitals to determine levels of satisfaction and loyalty, and we found serious concerns. At this point customers had already begun switching to competitors. Had senior executives used the "right" information from its sales force survey as a portent of trouble with its customers, it could have taken action early on to stem customer defection.

MYTH 4:
MEASUREMENT
CREATES REALITY

This myth usually surfaces when senior executives are in the process of deciding whether or not to gather information on a problem area. Take employee attitude surveys as an example. Many executives implicitly ascribe almost magical powers to surveys. This myth holds that by asking employees how they feel, you risk creating negative feelings. Never mind that these feelings may have been there all along. More than likely, management was simply unaware or unable to deal with them. At one global pharmaceutical company, after one survey revealed deep-seated morale problems in the work force, managers turned skittish and refused another round of surveys a year later. They didn't want to rock the boat. While ignorance may be bliss, it usually creates trouble. In this case, senior managers' reluctance only reinforced their image as being aloof and uncaring.

Smart companies know that information is the foundation for understanding and effective problem solving. A paper manufacturer held its breath as it conducted a company-wide employee survey. Executives were afraid that a potentially divisive pay issue would rear its ugly head. When the survey results were examined, pay issues were ranked fifth or lower in importance by the majority of workers. Safety and long-term job creation took priority. These findings helped management and the union avoid the usual contract gridlock and focus instead on finding common ground for the truly pressing issues.

MYTH 5:
MEASUREMENT
STIFLES CREATIVITY

For proof of the controlling power of this myth, just check the vision statement of the average company. We worked with a pharmaceutical company with a stated strategy that was studded with the usual pieties about its humanitarian mission, quality, innovative products, commitment to customers, and the great value placed on its people. (The fact that the company recently downsized by cutting people and slashing its R&D budget is quite another matter.) When we asked one senior executive about what guidance the strategy provided, his answer did not inspire great confidence. "Trying to get a handle on the strategy," he remarked, "is like sculpting fog." Had the top team thought through specific measurement criteria for its product and market categories, required capabilities, and revenue and profit expectations, the strategic fog would have cleared, making way for creative planning and implementation within an agreed-upon strategic framework.

MYTH 6:
MEASUREMENT IS
ANTI-HUMANISTIC

Many managers believe that measurement is just not people friendly. Measurement often conjures up visions of green-eyeshaded numbers crunchers who suffer from a kind of anthrophobia, as they pursue time

FROM MEASUREMENT MYTH TO MEASUREMENT MANAGED   177

and motion studies and operating efficiency. Real managers, so this line of reasoning goes, get paid to produce results through people, and people don't lend themselves to the rigors of metrics and quantitative analysis.

Few would argue with the notion that the managerial process is more art than science, but while it may be unpredictable, it should never be imprecise. Take an essential task of every manager, setting goals and providing a context for achieving them. Surely this is a uniquely human endeavor, but it is one in which measurement can play a vital role by helping to specify goals and motivating people to attain them by providing feedback on progress.

Years ago a study of fund-raising efforts in small towns was conducted. The study compared those towns that had a visible display of the money collected—we've all seen those large posterboard thermometers indicating progress—with those without a visible measure of success. Not surprisingly, towns that measured progress and shared it with the community exceeded the performance of those that did not. Measurement enhances human activity, not stymies it.

MYTH 7:
THE MORE MEASUREMENT
THE BETTER

This myth is a polar opposite of the others, and usually leads to measurement running amok. We mentioned earlier the IT department of a large financial institution that developed over 150 different measures to track performance. Few understood them, and no attempt was made to set priorities. Not surprisingly, many of the measures were never effectively put in place, and the data collected from many of the others remained in the desk drawers of managers.

In another case, a multibillion-dollar division of a Fortune 100 chemical company initiated a quality-assessment process. Reams of data were collected from an array of internal and external measures, but the data were never integrated, never effectively analyzed for strategic implications, and never used to set division priorities.

The number of metrics is less important than the process used to arrive at them. Forget quantity and focus instead on linking measures to strategic capabilities, marketplace needs, and customer expectations. And remember, involve those closest to the action in defining the measures and setting the targets!

FROM MEASUREMENT MYTHS TO MEASUREMENT MANAGED

If you want to enjoy the success of being a measurement-managed company, then begin by keeping the measurement myths in check in your organization. Here are three actions to take.

First, become a measurement advocate. Look for ways to puncture measurement myths whenever they surface. Create opportunities to educate your colleagues about the importance of managing by measuring. And don't forget to lead by example. Whether you are the CEO, or a divisional, functional, or unit executive, make sure your actions are guided by a set of balanced financial and nonfinancial strategic performance measures.

Second, promote understanding, not blame. Measurement provides a gold mine of information about results. Don't turn information into ammunition aimed at an underperforming manager. It is far more productive to use information gained from measurement to dissect performance gaps, assess causes, and take corrective action. Nothing kills a measurement effort faster than a wake of measurement victims.

Third, set strategic priorities. Measurement invariably raises the issues of accountability. Many managers shy away from measurement because they fear that it may expose a weakness or add to that Everest-sized pile of unresolved issues confronting them. "If they measure it, I'll be forced to deal with it," is a lament we've heard from dozens of managers. The result is to entrap managers in bureaucratic micromeasures and meaningless activities. Strategic measures need to reflect corporate or unit priorities; tactical, operational measures should support strategic priorities and measures. This way, you streamline your measurement effort and avoid creating a house divided, as managers and their employees pursue contradictory sets of objectives, operational plans, initiatives, and measures.

Take these three actions and you will be on your way to shattering measurement myths and joining the ranks of effective, measurement-managed organizations.

POSTSCRIPT ON ACTION

This book covered a great deal of terrain on how to extricate organizations from the measurement paradox by installing strategic measures in an organization. Make no mistake about it, becoming a measurement-managed organization is a 360-degree task that involves strategy and structure, culture and systems, capabilities and processes.

Ultimately, ideas are for action. To make sure reward follows effort, we conclude with an outline of key actions for successfully navigating each of the seventeen gates to measurement management, along with the red flags which can scuttle the effort.

1. Formulate clear process objectives.
   Red Flag: Beware of unrealistic expectations and programmatic solutions that misread the interests of stakeholders and the organization's readiness for change. Don't underestimate the effort needed to achieve a full return on your investment in a new measurement-managed organization.

2. Make sure there is fundamental alignment among top team members on the business strategy.
   Red Flag: Don't assume that just because your top team members have been working closely together for many years they agree on strategic direction.

3. Develop a well-articulated theory or model of the business.
   Red Flag: Beware of assumed causal connections about what drives customer satisfaction and business results. Even with high-level agreement on the strategy, interpretations of how to implement that strategy are likely to vary widely among the leadership.

4. Be sure that the organization's leaders are committed to the strategy and a new set of leadership behaviors.

   Red Flag: Watch out for lip-service leadership that remains uninvolved in the deployment of strategic performance measures and uncommitted to working within the requirements of the new measurement landscape.

5. Test the theory of the business.

   Red Flag: Don't assume the senior team knows with certainty what drives performance and productivity. The view from the top is often high up and far away.

6. Be sure measures are clearly defined, valid, and reliable.

   Red flag: Avoid measures that are overly complex, difficult to convey, and are unreliable sources of information for those who must live with and use them.

7. Set clear performance targets.

   Red Flag: Beware of measurement for measurement's sake. Measures not accompanied by targeted levels of performance have only half their power to challenge, motivate, and direct the workforce.

8. Identify and train process leaders throughout the organization.

   Red Flag: Guard against making measurement a "top management thing," separated from middle managers who drive performance. Choose "movers and shakers" throughout the organization to help develop and sell the process.

9. Agree on an optimal structure for cascading strategic performance measures through the organization.

   Red Flag: Beware of being seduced by the current structure when making this decision. Know which units and leaders will drive success. These are the groups that need strategic performance measures and action plans linked closely to the enterprise measures.

10. Communicate the strategy clearly throughout the organization.

    Red Flag: Don't demand strategies and measures from other employees before the top-of-the-house strategy is in order. Watch out for communication about the business strategy that remains just talk. Remember: Executive body language delivers the most potent message.

11. Train and support the leaders of the cascade effort.

    Red Flag: Don't assume a level of strategic and measurement sophistication. Managers down the line may know about operational measures. The odds are against them knowing much about designing and implementing a strategic measurement system.

12. Develop and link unit measures to one another and to the higher-level scorecard.

    Red Flag: Beware of "new math" or "hockey stick projections." When it comes to targets and measures, the sum of the supporting units should add up to the sum of the enterprise.

13. Link strategic performance measures to behaviors.

    Red Flag: Beware of crucial targets—especially short-term ones—that don't include a roadmap for reaching them. Ask for plans addressing key gaps from supporting units, teams, and individuals that are consistent with the "theory of the business."

14. Integrate the strategic performance measures with management of the business.

    Red Flag: Beware of measures that live in a drawer or fail to elicit passion. If no one talks or argues about a measure, no one cares. Also, beware of measures that don't drive some things off the plate. Prioritization means *not* doing some things.

15. Align human resource systems with the strategic performance measures.

    Red Flag: Watch for disconnects in how human performance is managed. Are your strategic performance objectives, reward and recognition systems, training and development plans aligned with one another—and with your measurement system? Remember: What you measure is what you'll get.

16. Link technology systems to the strategic performance measures.

    Red Flag: Beware of technology systems that start to assume a life of their own. The only purpose of such systems should be to make information available to managers when they want it and in a format they can understand. Sometimes less is more.

17. Continuously improve the theory of the business and the strategic performance measures.

    Red Flag: Beware of measures that change too much—and of measures that don't change enough. Be strategic in adjusting and improving measures.

LINKING HIGH-LEVEL STRATEGIC PERFORMANCE MEASURES TO THE DAY-TO-DAY BUSINESS

This appendix explores in greater detail our initial discussion of "linkage" for those seeking a deeper understanding of the subject.

Success in employing strategic performance measures depends heavily on the ability to establish linkages between high-level measures and the day-to-day running of the business. There are, in fact, two kinds of important linkages that the best measurement-managed companies are able to establish: initiative linkages and individual linkages.

Initiative linkage refers to the ability of an organization to evaluate the impact of specific initiatives on key performance areas within the model of the business; *individual linkage* refers to the ability of an organization to link the high-level strategic performance measures to the competencies and performance objectives of individual employees within the organizations. These two capabilities are crucial to an organization's ability to achieve maximum benefit from its strategic performance measures.

INITIATIVE LINKAGE

One of the greatest values of collecting and using strategic performance measures is having the ability to empirically test competing models or theories of the business held by executives. Without this, executives are left to engage in endless debates about direction and unproductive struggles for resources. By elaborating these theories in a graphical model, executives are able to see vividly where their theories conflict, and then empirically test them with the measurement system. Data help move the debate out of the political arena and bring final resolution to differences in perspective.

One of the most important—and potentially contentious—questions before every management team is: What actions or initiatives give us the greatest payoff? Strategic performance measures can help a management team answer this question.

For example, Figure A–1 represents the business model of a utility company with which we worked.* This utility had been collecting a wealth of employee, customer, operations, and financial data for many years, but these data had never been linked together. With adjustments to the company's data collection process to allow more effective performance matching among different departments, it became possible to develop a line of sight from customer satisfaction to employee commitment to specific human resource investments.

Statistical analysis of the utility's performance measures helped confirm three central product/service attributes that were drivers of customer satisfaction: fast problem resolution, billing accuracy, and knowledgeable employees. The analysis indicated that fast problem resolution was the strongest predictor of customer satisfaction, as indicated by the "S" in Figure A–1.

Additional analyses confirmed that the three customer drivers, in turn, were influenced by four people drivers—customer service employees' self confidence, product knowledge and service orientation, along with rewards for service—and several operations drivers. In this illustration, we will focus on the people drivers, though we could track a similar analysis for the operations drivers. Through additional statistical analysis, the utility was able to determine which people drivers had the strongest impact on the customer drivers. In this case, rewards for service proved to be the strongest predictor of problem resolution, which in turn was the strongest predictor of customer satisfaction. One hypothesized people measure, employee self-confidence,

---

*The examples discussed in this appendix are based on real-life experiences. However, we have modified the models and measured relationships to maintain client confidentiality.

Figure A–1 Utility Company's Theory of the Business

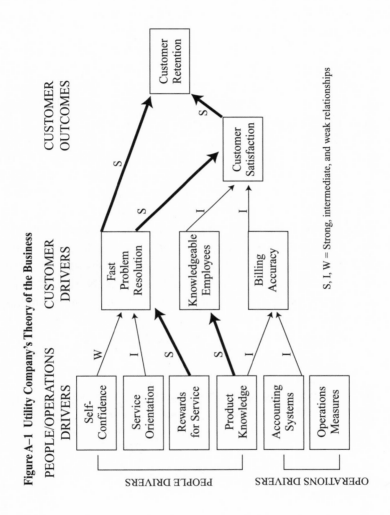

187

had only a weak relationship with problem resolution and was subsequently removed from consideration as an area worthy of major investments.

Once the utility validated that these three people drivers had the largest impact on customers' satisfaction, it became possible to evaluate the likely impact of specific initiatives on the people drivers first, and then ultimately on customer satisfaction and retention.

Table A–1 lists five new initiatives that were launched during the previous year to address gaps in the three people drivers. Subsequently, executives at the utility examined the impact of each of these initiatives on their model. They found, for example, that product training had a strong impact on product knowledge, which in turn had a strong influence on customers' perceptions of knowledgeable employees (Figure A–1). Similarly, the new service orientation program had a strong impact on service orientation scores on the employee survey, which in turn had an intermediate impact on fast problem resolution (again, see Figure A–1).

To illustrate the full linkage—from initiatives to drivers—let's look at "fast problem resolution," the strongest driver of customer satisfaction. Low scores in the utility's measure of "fast problem resolution" were found to have a strong link to customer satisfaction ratings. As shown in Figure A–1, service orientation and rewards for service both contributed to problem resolution speed, with rewards for service being the stronger predictor.

Looking first at service orientation in Table A–1, it is clear that four of the five initiatives were having some impact on this people driver, with

Table A–1: LINKING ORGANIZATION INITIATIVES TO PEOPLE DRIVERS

	People Drivers		
Initiatives	**Service Orientation**	**Rewards for Service**	**Product Knowledge**
Product Training			S
Service Orientation Program	S		
Values Training	W		
Service Recognition Program	W	W	
360° Feedback	S	W	I

S,I,W = Strong, Intermediate, Weak relationships

the service orientation training and 360-degree feedback initiatives having the strongest effect. In contrast, only two initiatives were having any impact on rewards for service—the most important driver of problem resolution speed, and in turn, customer satisfaction. This suggested that a different set of initiatives would be needed to address deficiencies in the "rewards for service" driver.

An alternative approach to evaluating the impact of initiative investments is to examine the impact of different initiatives across multiple drivers. As shown in Table A–1, neither the values training nor the service recognition program were having much of an impact on the three people drivers. In contrast, the 360-degree feedback process was having an impact on all three people drivers. The analysis points to the potential leverage that can be obtained from certain initiatives as compared to others. In making such evaluations, it is also necessary to examine the level of investment required by each initiative.

Once a company has created linkages from high-level outcomes to drivers to initiatives, sets of initiatives can be evaluated, as illustrated in Table A–2, which shows how an organization can evaluate the effectiveness of its initiatives, and in most cases reduce their number, while increasing the impact of those that are retained. Without such an analysis, managers are forced to juggle priorities on "a wing and a prayer," hoping that the initiatives they focus on will have a significant impact on their bottom line.

One of the greatest advantages of deploying strategic performance measures is the enhanced ability to tie together multiple business activities. This can help eliminate low-value activities, provide a basis for better resource allocation, and serve as a common accountability mechanism that integrates activities across the business. None of these elements are necessarily new to businesses. However, strategic performance measures provide a tool to help integrate often dimly perceived elements into a cohesive framework that links cause and effect.

Initiative linkage can also be done for internal service units and, in the process, help to address an increasingly asked question: What real value are internal service organizations adding to the business?

Figure A–2 shows part of the value chain for an information technology group in a financial services company. The group hypothesized a relationship between its functional performance and the overall business performance as seen by external customers.

Table A–2: LINKING RESULTS, DRIVERS, AND INITIATIVES

Results	Drivers				Actions	
Customer Results	Customer Drivers (SPMs)	Perf.	People Drivers (SPMs)	Perf.	Initiatives	Impact
• Customer Retention	• Problem Resolution	L	• Rewards for Service (S)	L	• Service Recognition Program	W
					• 360° Feedback	W
			• Service Orientation (I)	M	• Service Training	S
					• Values Training	W
					• Service Recognition Program	W
					• 360° Feedback	S
• Customer Satisfaction	• Knowledgeable Employees	M	• Product Knowledge (S)	M	• Product Training	S
					• 360° Feedback	I
	• Billing Accuracy	H	• Accounting Systems (S)	M	• No actions taken	—
			• Product Knowledge (S)	M	• Product Training	S
					• 360° Feedback	I

S,I,W = Strong, intermediate, weak impact
H,M,L = High, medium, low performance

By statistically analyzing both the high-level and department measures over several periods, the group was able to show that for every 10 percent improvement in commitment of its own employees, IT was able to realize an 8 percent increase in perceptions of value by its internal customers. Furthermore, this 8 percent improvement could be related to a 1.5 percent increase in perceived valued by external customers.

INDIVIDUAL LINKAGE

In the end, the success or failure of organizations depends on the actions of individual employees. To be truly effective, strategic performance measures need to be linked directly to the day-to-day activities of people in the organization. An important way for this to happen is to link strategic measures to the competencies and the performance objectives of individual employees.

Figure A–2 Linkage Analysis for a 10% improvement in It Employee Commitment Scores

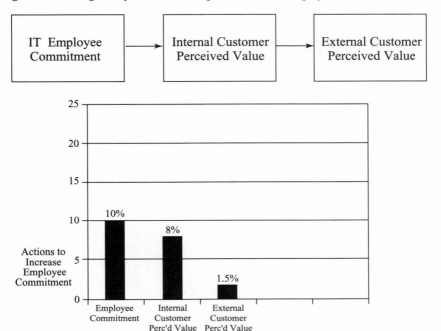

Figure A–3 provides a graphical overview of how Factex linked its strategic performance measures to individual objectives and accountabilities. Tables A–3 through A–5 give more detailed information about how the linkages were achieved.

Table A–3 summarizes the way in which the strategic performance measures were cascaded down to individuals within the account management department. The account management function has a direct influence on Factex's strategic performance measures in areas such as client retention, revenue growth, employee commitment, and internal value, but it does not significantly contribute to new business or to new target-market bidding opportunities. Notice that both account executives and the account executive managers contribute to client retention and revenue growth. However, because account executive managers have responsibility for the commitment, growth, and learning of the account executives reporting to

Figure A–3 Linking Organizational, Functional, and Individual Strategic Performance Measures

Table A–3: LINE OF SIGHT FROM COMPANY STRATEGIC PERFORMANCE MEASURES TO INDIVIDUAL ACCOUNTABILITIES

Company Strategic Measures	Account Management Department Measures	Position Measures	
		Account Executive	Account Executive Manager
New business	N/A	N/A	N/A
Client retention	X	X	X
Credit quality	X	X	X
Revenue growth	X	X	X
Growth/Learning	X		X
Employee commitment	X		X
Internal customer value	X	X	X
Target market bidding opportunities	N/A	N/A	N/A

Table A–4: INDIVIDUAL ACCOUNT EXECUTIVE MEASURES

Company Area	Market Outcome		
	Account Management Department Measure	1996 Baseline	1997 Target
Client retention	Number of controllable terminations as a percentage of client portfolio	3.4	2.5
	Percentage of total revenue lost	4.7	3.0

them, these two measures are on the account managers' scorecard, but not on that of the account executives.

Table A–4 illustrates how one strategic performance measure, client retention, is translated into a measure for the account management department. At Factex, account executives play a key role in quarterbacking the overall relationship with a client, and in this position have the greatest influence over controllable terminations. As part of the measurement cascading process, the account management department at Factex assumed responsibility for reducing controllable terminations from a baseline of 3.4 percent to a target of 2.5 percent and reducing revenue lost from terminations from 4.7 percent to 3.0 percent.

Finally, Table A–5 shows a set of measures for the account management department that is directly related to the accountabilities of an individual account executive. Continuing the example of client terminations, account executives have responsibilities, as part of their individual accountabilities, for negotiating contract renewals, providing forty-eight-hour problem solving, and thirty-days-or-better resolution of dialogues with clients on issues such as building lending programs and reviewing account information.

In sum, Tables A–3 through A–5 depict the linkage that connects the corporate strategic performance measures to individual accountabilities. When such linkage is coupled with effective accountability discussions, ongoing coaching, and regular feedback, it becomes a powerful system for aligning day-to-day behaviors with the overarching strategic business objectives.

In Chapter 8, we briefly discussed the way in which Factex developed account executive accountabilities linked to their corporate strategic performance measures. The way in which strategy, strategic measurement, and core competencies can successfully interlink and build on one another is further illustrated by our recent experience with a high-tech firm positioned to provide customized computer hardware to a specialized market niche. In the course of reviewing its strategy, the firm realized that it did not have the technological capabilities to go head-to-head on product innovation with larger players. However, in assessing the marketplace, an important gap in service delivery was identified. By combining niche expertise with long-term relationships, executives believed they could differentiate themselves

Table A–5: LINK BETWEEN ACCOUNT EXECUTIVE DEPARTMENT
MEASURES AND INDIVIDUAL ACCOUNTABILITIES

Account Management Department Measures	Individual Account Executive Accountabilities
Client retention	• Negotiate contract renewals • Problem solving: 48-hour response • Proactive account servicing (30-day dialogues)
Credit quality	• Partner with credit department to ensure less than 2% of portfolio lost
Revenue growth	• Secure premium pricing • Introduce new/modified services

through highly customized service. This, in turn, meant giving up the firm's "product innovation" tradition for a new "service" mentality.

The strategic measurement system was crucial in helping this company track the development of its new service capability. Here are the steps the company followed in using measurement to change its culture:

- First, the firm identified which functions and roles were key to an improved service mentality. Certainly, front-line sales and customer service reps were essential. But there were other key roles. High-level customer service meant responsive and individualized service from the finance and accounting departments as well. It also meant that the marketing department would need to project a new service image.
- Once identified, the critical competencies were captured in both high-level and supporting strategic metrics. For example, at a high level, new service measures were included in a revamped market survey that assessed service perceptions of both existing and potential customers. Bradley Gale's measure of market perceived value was used to gauge the perceived value of this company's services versus those of the competition. The survey helped the organization determine: (1) if service, versus other attributes such as price and product innovation, was important enough to provide differentiation in the marketplace; and (2) where the company stood relative to the competition on the all-important service dimension. This high-level metric enabled executives to learn whether or not their strategy was viable and how far they needed to travel to implement it. Equally as important, the metric provided a means of communicating to the organization what was important and where the company stood relative to developing a crucial new competency.
- Next, the high-level market-perceived value metric was translated into functional measures to allow different units of the organization to assess their progress in developing key functional competencies. For example, since problem solving and response speed were seen as two highly valued service attributes, measures for each were incorporated into the measures of the customer service department. There, they provided tactical guidance for employees' service improvement efforts.

- As a next step, the various metrics were tied to the selection, placement, and development systems. First, competency gaps were identified based on the performance gaps in both the high-level and the functional measures. These competency gaps were then translated into specific plans for recruitment, selection, placement, and training.
- Finally, the organization continued to refine the measurement system at both the global and functional levels. For example, information from early customer surveys was used to eliminate items that tracked marginally important service attributes, thereby focusing the survey more on the service issues that were most important to the customer.

The use of measurement helped this organization translate a new strategy into a marketplace reality in the least amount of time. The measurement system first helped articulate exactly what the new strategy involved and then got everyone to participate in tracking how well the change in direction was being implemented.

The main challenge today does not lie in the richness and robustness of ideas about future strategic direction, but in making these ideas sufficiently specific and relevant so they can be implemented by every employee. Strategy happens when everyone's performance is tied to its success.

Measurement plays a pivotal role in linking business strategy to day-to-day operational planning and decision making. There are organizations that understand the importance of strategic measurement but never reap the full rewards because the measures remain at too high a level. They remain trapped in the measurement paradox. The real action starts when strategy and measurement leave the boardroom and work their way into the depths of the organization to direct, focus, and align all employees.

NOTES

PART I INTRODUCTION
1. H. James Harrington, *Business Process Improvement: The Breakthrough Strategy for Total Quality, Productivity, and Competitiveness* (New York: McGraw-Hill, 1991).
2. Anthony J. Rucci, Steven P. Kirn, and Richard T. Quinn, "The Employee-Customer Profit Chain at Sears," *Harvard Business Review,* January/February 1998.
3. Gordon Bethune, with Scott Huler, *From Worst to First: Behind the Scenes of Continental's Remarkable Comeback* (New York: John Wiley & Sons, 1998).
4. Brian S. Morgan and William A. Schiemann, "Measuring People and Performance: Closing the Gap," *Quality Progress,* January 1999.
5. John H. Lingle and William A. Schiemann, "From Balanced Scorecard to Strategic Gauges: Is Measurement Worth It?" *Management Review,* March 1996.

CHAPTER 1
1. William A. Schiemann, "Organizational Change: Lessons From a Turnaround," *Management Review,* April 1992, pp. 34–37.
2. Robert S. Kaplan and David P. Norton, "The Balanced Scorecard—Measures That Drive Performance," *Harvard Business Review,* January-February 1992, pp. 71–79.
3. Brian S. Morgan and William A. Schiemann, "Measuring People and Performance: Closing the Gap," *Quality Progress,* January 1999.
4. John H. Lingle and William A. Schiemann, "Is Data Scatter Subverting Your Strategy?" *Management Review,* May 1994, pp. 53–58.
5. William A. Schiemann, "Why Change Fails," *Across The Board,* April 1992, pp. 53–54.
6. Dave Ulrich and Dale Lake, *Organizational Capability: Competing from the Inside Out,* (New York: John Wiley & Sons, 1990); Jack W. Wiley, "Linking

Survey Results to Customer Satisfaction and Business Performance," in Allen I. Kraut (Ed.), *Organizational Surveys: Tools for Assessment and Change* (San Francisco: Jossey-Bass, 1996), pp. 330–359; William A. Schiemann, "Driving Change Through Surveys: Aligning Employees, Customers, and Other Key Stakeholders," in Allen I. Kraut (Ed.), *Organizational Surveys,* pp. 88–116.

7. Anthony J. Rucci, Steven P. Kirn, and Richard T. Quinn, "The Employee-Customer-Profit Chain at Sears," *Harvard Business Review,* January/February 1998, pp. 82–97.

CHAPTER 2

1. Sam M. Malone, Jr., "The Xerox Management Model: Aligning Performance Across the Organization," (New Orleans, February 1998, International Quality & Productivity Center Performance Measurement for Strategic Planning Conference).

2. Anthony J. Rucci, Steven P. Kirn, and Richard T. Quinn, " The Employee-Customer-Profit Chain at Sears," *Harvard Business Review,* January-February 1998, pp. 82–97.

3. Gordon Bethune, *From Worst to First* (New York: John Wiley & Sons, 1998).

4. Stan Davis, *Future Perfect* (New York: Addison Wesley Longman, 1997).

5. Tracy Kidder, *Soul of a New Machine* (New York: Avon Books, 1995).

6. John P. Kotter and James L. Heskett, *Corporate Culture and Performance* (New York: Free Press, 1992).

7. Corporate Strategy Board, *Unbroken Growth: Salient Insights from Inaugural Research,* 1997.

8. Ray Marshall and Marc Tucker, *Thinking for a Living* (New York: Basic Books, 1993), p. 35.

CHAPTER 3

1. Bradley Gale, *Managing Customer Value* (New York: Free Press, 1994).

2. Pamphlet entitled *Customers Mean Business: Surveys Show You Have More Dissatisfied Customers Than You Think,* published by the Direct Selling Education Foundation, 1982.

3. Edgar H. Schein, "Organizational Culture," *American Psychologist, 45,* No. 2 (February 1990), 109–119.

CHAPTER 4

1. Terry D. Anderson, Ron Ford, and Marilyn Hamilton, *Transforming Leadership* (Winter Park, Florida: Saint Lucie Press, 1998).

2. Howard M. Fischer, Wharton School of Business, "Conference on Leadership Capabilities for Winning Companies," Philadelphia, June 1998.

3. A. G. Greenwald, "Cognitive Learning, Cognitive Response to Persuasion, and Attitude Change." In A. G. Greenwald, T. C. Brock, and T. Ostrom

(Eds.), *Psychological Foundations of Attitudes* (San Diego: Academic Press), pp. 147–170.

4. L. Festinger and J. M. Carlsmith, "Cognitive Consequences of Forced Compliance." *Journal of Abnormal and Social Psychology, 58* (1959), 203–210.

5. M. E. Losch and J. T. Cacioppo, "Cognitive Dissonance May Enhance Sympathetic Tonus, but Attitudes Are Changed to Reduce Negative Effect Rather Than Arousal." *Journal of Experimental Social Psychology, 26* (1990), 289–304.

6. Edgar H. Schein, "Organizational Culture," *American Psychologist, 45,* No. 2 (February 1990), 109–119.

7. L. Festinger and J. M. Carlsmith, "Cognitive Consequences of Forced Compliance," *op. cit.*

PART II INTRODUCTION

1. William A. Schiemann, "Why Change Fails," *Across the Board,* April 1992, pp. 53–54.

CHAPTER 5

1. William A. Schiemann, "Why Change Fails," *Across the Board,* April 1992, pp. 53–54.

CHAPTER 6

1. James C. Collins and Jerry I. Porras, *Built to Last* (New York: Harper Business, 1997), p. 368.

CHAPTER 8

1. Gordon Bethune, *From Worst to First* (New York: John Wiley & Sons), p. 234.

2. Homans, G., "Group Factors in Work Productivity," in H. Proshansky and B. Seidenberg, eds., *Basic Studies in Social* Psychology (New York: Holt, Rinehart & Winston, 1965), pp. 592–604.

3. Joseph L. Rosenberger, "Answers Are Easy," *Across the Board,* April 1997.

INDEX